Conversations with S. J. Perelman

Literary Conversations Series

Peggy Whitman Prenshaw
General Editor

Conversations
with S. J. Perelman

Edited by
Tom Teicholz

University Press of Mississippi
Jackson

Copyright © 1995 by the University Press of Mississippi
All rights reserved
Manufactured in the United States of America

98 97 96 95   4 3 2 1

The paper in this book meets the guidelines for permanence and durability of the
Committee on Production Guidelines for Book Longevity of the Council on Library
Resources.

Library of Congress Cataloging-in-Publication Data

Perelman, S. J. (Sidney Joseph), 1904–1979
    Conversations with S. J. Perelman / edited by Tom Teicholz.
        p. cm. — (Literary conversations series)
    Includes index.
    ISBN 0-87805-789-7 (cloth). — ISBN 0-87805-790-0 (paper)
    1. Perelman, S. J. (Sidney Joseph), 1904–1979—Interviews.
2. Humorists, American—20th century—Interviews. 3. Authors,
American—20th century—Interviews. I. Teicholz, Tom. II. Title.
III. Series.
PS3531.E6544Z464   1995
818′.5209—dc20   94-42526
                                                                          CIP

British Library Cataloging-in-Publication data available

Works by S. J. Perelman

Fiction & Essays

Dawn Ginsbergh's Revenge. Horace Liveright, Inc., New York, 1929.
Parlor, Bedlam and Bath (with Quentin Reynolds). Horace Liveright, Inc., New York, 1930.
Strictly from Hunger. Random House, New York, 1937.
Look Who's Talking!. Random House, New York, 1940.
The Dream Department. Random House, New York, 1943.
Crazy Like a Fox. Random House, New York, 1944.
Keep It Crisp. Random House, New York, 1946.
The Best of S. J. Perelman. Random House, New York, 1947.
Acres and Pains. Reynal and Hitchcock, New York, 1947.
Westward Ha!. Simon and Schuster, New York, 1948.
Listen to the Mocking Bird. Simon and Schuster, New York, 1949.
The Swiss Family Perelman. Simon and Schuster, New York, 1950.
The Ill-Tempered Clavichord. Simon and Schuster, New York, 1952.
Perelman's Home Companion. Simon and Schuster, New York, 1955.
The Road to Miltown. Simon and Schuster, New York, 1957.
The Most of S. J. Perelman. Simon and Schuster, New York, 1958.
The Rising Gorge. Simon and Schuster, New York, 1961.
Chicken Inspector #23. Simon and Schuster, New York, 1966.
Baby, It's Cold Inside. Simon and Schuster, New York, 1970.
Vinegar Puss. Simon and Schuster, New York, 1975.
Eastward Ha!. Simon and Schuster, New York, 1977.
The Last Laugh. Simon and Schuster, New York, 1981.

Screenplays

Monkey Business. Paramount, 1931.
Horse Feathers. Paramount, 1932.
Hold 'Em Jail. RKO, 1932.
Sitting Pretty. Paramount, 1933.
The Big Broadcast of 1936 (uncredited). Paramount, 1935.
Sweethearts (uncredited). MGM, 1938.
Ambush. Paramount, 1939.
Boy Trouble. Paramount, 1939.
The Golden Fleecing. MGM, 1940.
Around the World in 80 Days. United Artists, 1956.

Plays

The Third Little Show, 1931.
Walk a Little Faster, 1932.
All Good Americans (with Laura Perelman), 1933.

The Night before Christmas (with Laura Perelman), 1941.
One Touch of Venus (with Ogden Nash), 1943.
Sweet Bye and Bye (with Al Hirschfeld), 1946.
The Beauty Part, Samuel French, New York, 1962.

Contents

Introduction

The writing of S. J. Perelman has caused many people to laugh, some so hard they fell off their chairs. I should know: it happens to me whenever I crack open a volume. I can't remember the first time I came across Perelman's pastiche of Anglophilic precision and Yiddish patois—it was no doubt in the pages of *The New Yorker,* but since then I smile at the mere mention of his name.

The interviews herein collected span Perelman's entire career. The first was published in 1933 and the last appeared posthumously in 1979. In between Perelman moved blithely from writing for the theater to movies to television and back to movies punctuated by many collections of his humor and travel writing. Though Perelman was no actor, it was clear that he was a performer and that the S. J. Perelman of these interviews, the professional curmudgeon, was a character of his own invention.

As he tells us in these interviews Sidney Joseph Perelman began his professional life as a cartoonist in the style of John Held, Jr., but quickly switched to the short comic pieces he is known for.

Perelman thought of himself as writing in a tradition: he was inspired, we learn, by George Ade, Stephen Leacock and Ring Lardner. Humor was his vocation. "Humor," he tells one interviewer, "is purely a point of view and only the pedants try to classify it. For me its chief merit is the use of the unexpected, the glancing allusion, the deflation of pomposity and the constant repetition of one's helplessness in a majority of situations."

Not that Perelman found his own material that funny: "Let me assure you I don't sit in the chimney cackling over what I've written," he tells us. For Perelman the challenge was in having the right target to vent his talent on. Over the years he brought his sensibility to bear on a wide variety of topics. In the beginning, Perelman confides to William Zinsser in the *New York Times Magazine,* he was "preoccupied with advertising, and then trade magazines." The magazine of the oral hygiene industry was a particular favorite. He then went on a nostalgia kick revisiting the books and films of his youth such as *Pollyanna, The Mystery of Dr. Fu Manchu* and *Scaramouche*. This produced his collection *Cloud-land Revisited*.

Travel was a particularly good source for Perelman. The worse the conditions he found himself in, the more he could put it to good comic effect. Or as Perelman himself put it more succinctly: "Misery breeds copy."

In 1927 Perelman and his wife Laura first travelled to Paris and they returned as often as possible. Nonetheless his career as a grand adventurer began in earnest in 1947 when he embarked on an around-the-world trip with cartoonist Al Hirschfeld that led to *Westward Ha!* A few years later he circled the globe again this time *en famille*. This trip led to the hilarious *Swiss Family Perelman*. Over the years he circled the globe more than six times and his adventures included tagging along with an all-woman safari in East Africa and retracing Phileas Fogg's footsteps around the world. Towards the end of his life he even drove his cherished MG roadster across the European and Asian continent retracing the route of the Paris to Peking rally.

"I've lived in a number of places in my life," he says in an interview entitled "The Writer as Celebrity" by Maralyn Lois Polak, "and can't make up my mind which is the most agreeable. I enjoy travel so much, but I find most places after a lengthy stay have drawbacks. So the idea is to be a moving target. Then it's impossible for people to pick you off."

Perelman said the great motivator for writing was always the landlord. In his lifelong attempt to secure easy money, Perelman found himself in Hollywood where he wrote scripts over the course of more than three decades. He was not particularly fond of the place and his descriptions of his work there surface in the interviews as some of his more practiced routines. He tells Ms. Polak that "Hollywood is a dreary industrial town controlled by hoodlums of enormous wealth." He credits Dorothy Parker with saying that Hollywood dispensed fairy money that seemed to evaporate as it crossed back East.

It was the Marx Brothers who first brought the Perelmans to Hollywood. Over the course of the interviews herein collected we

begin to understand the scope of his love-hate relationship with the
Marx brothers in general and Groucho in particular. We see how
it pains him that every interview must dwell on the short time he
spent in the 1930s with the brothers Marx. But when he and
Groucho meet in London for a session with Kenneth Tynan, we see
the respect and admiration each held for the other.

The Perelman that emerges from these interviews develops from
cynic to curmudgeon. We read as he becomes progressively
sickened with New York and the United States. He doesn't like
profanity in writing and full frontal nudity in movies. We read as
he leaves the United States for England; and then we read of his
return. At times we hear that he is writing his autobiography,
''The Hindsight Saga'' and then at a later stage we learn that he
could not get past page thirty-five.

Perelman's great ability was to take the tired English language
and make of it something new and shiny to be appreciated all
over again. We watch as many of his interviewers fall into his
jargon. But for all Perelman's anglophilia, we see his affection for
corned beef and for the joys of Yiddish. As he told one interviewer,
''There are nineteen words in Yiddish that convey gradations of
disparagement from a mild, fluttery helplessness to a state of
downright, irreconcilable brutishness. All of them can be usefully
employed to pinpoint the kind of individuals I write about.''

People often ask why Perelman never wrote a novel, but he
explains to one interviewer that he views himself as a miniaturist,
saying: ''For the past thirty-four years I have been approached
almost hourly by damp people with foreheads like Rocky Ford
melons who urge me to knock off my frivolous writing career and
get started on that novel I'm burning to write. I have no earthly
intention of doing any such thing. I don't believe in the importance
of scale. To me the muralist is no more valid than the miniature
painter. In this very large country, where size is all and where
Thomas Wolfe outranks Robert Benchley, I am content to stitch
away at my embroidery hoop. I think the form I work in can have
its own distinction and I would like to surpass what I have done
in it.''

There is no question that Perelman succeeded at being a unique
practitioner of an artform that he himself made distinctive. He may

have his models and his imitators, but he is the *non-pareil*. Perelman characterized his writing style as "a mixture of all the trash I read as a child, all the clichés, criminal slang, liberal doses of Yiddish, and some of what I learned in school from impatient teachers." But a better description was proffered by William Shawn, the editor of the *New Yorker,* who said of Perelman, "He was a master of the English language, and no one had put the language to more stunning comic effect than he did."

As with other books in the Literary Conversations series, the interviews are reprinted uncut. Although there is inevitably a certain amount of repetition, no two interviews are exactly alike, and each contributes to the portrait of this delightful humorist.

TT
August 1994

Chronology

1904   Sidney Joseph Perelman is born on February 1, in Brooklyn, New York, to Joseph and Sophie Perelman. The family Perelman moves to Providence, Rhode Island.

1921–25 Attends Brown University; contributes cartoons to the college humor magazine *The Brown Jug.*

1922   Meets transfer student Nathan Weinstein (Nathanael West).

1924   Publishes first humor pieces in *The Brown Jug* and *Casements,* a student literary magazine; is elected editor of *The Brown Jug.*

1925   Perelman leaves Brown three credits short of graduation; receives a contract as a cartoonist for *Judge,* a national humor magazine; moves to New York. Harold Ross, who later founded *The New Yorker,* is co-editor.

1929   Marries 18-year-old Lorraine Weinstein (Nathanael's sister), by then known as Laura West; honeymoon in France. Perelman's first book, *Dawn Ginsbergh's Revenge,* is published, containing 49 pieces, the majority of which were written for *Judge.*

1930   Starts writing for *College Humor,* "the magazine with a college education," edited by H. N. Swanson, who would later be Perelman's agent. *Parlor, Bedlam and Bath,* a novel written with Quentin Reynolds, is published. The Perelmans spend the summer in Europe; Perelman's work first appears in *The New Yorker.* Perelman attends a performance of the Marx Brothers' Broadway play, *Animal Crackers;* sends Groucho a note during intermission; Groucho invites the Perelmans backstage after the show; invites Perelman to write a radio script; a few days later when Perelman tells him his idea for the four brothers to be stowaways aboard an ocean liner, Groucho remarks, "This is too good to waste on a radio show—it's going to be our next picture." The Perelmans are off to Hollywood.

1930–32   Perelman works as one of the writers on two Marx Brothers movies, *Monkey Business* and *Horse Feathers*. Perelman also contributes sketches to the Broadway revues "Third Little Show" and "Walk a Little Faster."

1932   The Perelmans purchase their home in Bucks County, Pennsylvania. The Perelmans return to Hollywood to work on a number of movies.

1933   The Screenwriter's Guild is formed by several of the Perelmans' good friends; Laura serves on the executive committee.

1935   *All Good Americans,* a play by Sid and Laura Perelman, appears on Broadway. The Perelmans become contract screenwriters for MGM under Irving Thalberg.

1936   Adam Perelman is born; the Perelmans move back East. S. J. Perelman works with Ogden Nash on screen adaptation of Dale Carnegie's *How to Win Friends and Influence People.*

1937   Random House publishes *Strictly from Hunger,* 21 pieces including "Waiting for Santy," a takeoff of Clifford Odet's "Waiting for Lefty." Back to Hollywood on MGM payroll.

1938   Daughter Abby is born. Working on screenplay for *Ambush* and *Boy Trouble.*

1940   *Look Who's Talking* is published by Random House. Nathanael West and his wife Eileen die in a car crash on December 22.

1941   The Perelman's play *The Night before Christmas* closes after a run of only 22 performances (later became the film *Larceny, Inc.*).

1943   *The Dream Department,* containing many pieces from the *New Yorker,* is published. Perelman hailed as "the funniest man in America." The play "A Touch of Venus," a musical comedy by Perelman and Ogden Nash and starring Mary Martin, opens on Broadway and is a great success.

1944   Random House publishes *Crazy Like a Fox,* which becomes a bestseller.

1946   *Keep It Crisp* is published; includes Perelman's takeoff on Raymond Chandler, "Farewell My Lovely Appetizer."

1947   *Acres and Pains,* Perelman's book about country living, is published. Perelman and Al Hirschfeld leave for their trip around the world.

1949   *Listen to the Mocking Bird* is published by Simon & Schuster. Perelman embarks on another around the world trip, this time with his family, which leads to *The Swiss Family Perelman.*

1952   *The Ill-Tempered Clavichord* is published.

1954   Perelman's six part series on East Africa, "Dr. Perelman, I Presume or Small-Bore in Africa," appears in *The New Yorker.*

1955   Perelman commences work on screenplay for *Around the World in 80 Days.*

1956   *Around the World in 80 Days* opens to great acclaim. Perelman wins the New York Film Critics Award for his screen adaptation, as well as an Academy Award (along with John Farrow and James Poe).

1957   *The Road to Miltown* is published; it receives a front page *New York Times* book review by Dorothy Parker and becomes a bestseller; works on "The Big Wheel" starring Bert Lahr for the "Omnibus" television program.

1958   Perelman is formally inducted into The National Institute of Arts and Letters. *The Most of S. J. Perelman,* a comprehensive collection of his works, is published.

1959   "Malice In Wonderland," consisting of three Hollywood cameos, appears on the "Omnibus" program.

1961   *The Rising Gorge* is published.

1962   *The Beauty Part* opens on Broadway starring Bert Lahr and Larry Hagman.

1963   Perelman serves as a writer on television program "Elizabeth Taylor's London."

1965   Perelman is awarded an honorary degree from Brown University.

1966   *Chicken Inspector #23* is published.

1970   Laura Perelman dies at age 58 on April 10. Perelman sells the farm and moves to England. His departure creates great controversy and great press.

1971   On March 5, Perelman leaves from the Reform Club in London to retrace Phileas Fogg's footsteps in *Around the World in Eighty Days*.

1972   Perelman returns to New York.

1975   *Vinegar Puss* is published. Sets off on sixth global tour.

1978   Receives special achievement medal at National Book Awards ceremony; decides to drive from Paris to Peking, tries to write series of articles about trip but never does.

1979   Perelman dies of a heart attack on October 17.

1981   Publication of *The Last Laugh,* Perelman's posthumous collection.

Conversations with S. J. Perelman

Who Are the Perelmans?

The New York Times / 1933

The New York Times, 10 December 1933. Copyright © 1933 by
The New York Times Company. Reprinted by permission.

The scene was a subterranean chamber in West Forty-fifth Street,
the time midnight, and a reporter with a fey and smoking curiosity
about such random and incongruous items as Bolivia's foreign
policy, the Holy Grail, Genghis Khan, Gertrude Stein and French
vermouth thought that he might putty up a few chinks in the armor
of his experience by tracking down the Perelmans, man and wife
and Brown graduates, and browbeating from them a confession as
to how authors feel with an opening only half an hour behind
them.

Accompanied by two native bearers and a spent Mormon carrying
the ecstatic news from Utah—for this was last Tuesday—the
reporter skirted the line of pedestrian bon vivants littering up
Broadway and presently found himself in the presence of Admiral
Courtney Burr, as intrepid a sailor as ever freebooted on the
Spanish Main. In the Admiral's atelier, underneath the same stage
upon which his bogus mariners boast and brawl, a stilly quiet
reigned. It was a quiet broken only by Fred Keating doing an imitation
of Harry Richman, the Admiral singing snatches from *Pinafore,*
Hope Williams defending Moses, the Sealyham, against charges
of stage conduct unbecoming an officer and a gentleman, two
hussars from the commissary department arguing about who should
have brought the opener and the ruction arising from a private
shambles in the corner between conflicting groups of ticket
brokers.

"Hobson, there was a sailor for you," said the Admiral as he
adjusted his cutlass and addressed the reporter with a show of
feeling. "It isn't every bluejacket who gets a chance to sink the
Merrimac in Manila Bay and come back on his shield under a blanket
of rotogravure clippings. Or did they have rotogravure clippings in
those grim and Spanish days, or am I thinking of Lee Tracy?"

3

"They didn't and it was another bay," muttered one of his equerries as he motioned to Felix for another piece of ice.

The Admiral ignored the interruption and went on his briny way. "I'm thinking of reproducing the whole thing on the lagoon in Central Park next summer. It would put all of Equity's personnel on the payroll, inflate recruiting and win the unqualified support of the entire Republican party. Remember, men, it was during a Republican administration that Hobson did his stuff. Call Chamberlain Brown in the morning. There's probably a Hobson gnawing his knuckles there this very minute."

"I think," ventured Hope Williams, "that the man is looking for someone." She indicated the reporter by waving the Sealyham at him.

"Speak up, mate, speak up," snorted the Admiral. "When the tang of the sea gets in my nostrils and the deep starts to roll and bound, there's no holding me. But if you think I have any orchestra seats for *Sailor Beware,* you're as mad as an adagio dancer. But I'll do a hornpipe for you at the first flutter of a woodwind!"

"It isn't tickets I want, it's the Perelmans," piped the investigator. "Didn't they write *All Good Americans,* the show that opened at the Henry Miller's tonight? I want to get their reactions to the audience, those gypsy serenaders in the pit, Sean O'Casey and the critics."

"That's Perelman," said the Admiral, smiling benignly on a small man in glasses, "and that's his wife. She's Laura to us and to Sid, and she wouldn't give you so much as a drachma for a Lucy Stoner. Sid's the phobe and Laura's the phile of the merger. They're both out of debt. Sid once did a handstand on the stairs leading up to the Trocadero, and they own a farm that they bought from Michael Gold."

A little baffled at the Admiral's imagery, the reporter beckoned to the playwrights and they followed him to the chaise lounge, where, once Mr. Keating had finished with Harry Richman, he began his heckling.

"What's your play about?" he asked more brightly than he looked.

"It's about our expatriates in Paris," said the male Perelman. "You know! All tangled up with love, liquor and loneliness,

excursions to Malmaison and Chantilly, forgetting all about it at the
Rotonde, and figuring out the rate of exchange. Sometimes I think
it's like *Oedipus Rex,* and sometimes I think it's like early O'Neill,
and once I thought it was like Jimmy Gleason.''

"What was like early O'Neill?" interrupted Laura.

"Beyond the Horizon," said Mr. Perelman, "and you'd be astonished to find out how people can spell Perelman. We're the
Perelmans with the single 'a.' Put two in it, and I'll have you hauled
up on charges.''

"Would I be overbold were I to ask you where you got the idea
for the play? Did it come to you the night like a vision or at noon
like lunch?''

"You lean toward the overbold, but we'll tell you," said Laura.
"A friend of ours was vacationing in Pernambuco. He sent us a
postal card and instead of showing the beach on Sunday it showed
a Brasillian coffee plantation. Now you go on from there.'' This
last to Sid.

"One look at the card and something started to surge within me,''
said Mr. Perelman. "The connotations of coffee. That was it.
French coffee lays our countrymen low. You are my countrymen,
aren't you? There was the plot. Now for the dialogue. For a
minute I got to thinking about the postcards that the man sells
outside the Cafe de la Paix, but I mastered my baser emotions
and decided that it must be a clean play.''

"There isn't anything in the play about crepes suzettes, is there?"
sallied the reporter, "or Pasteur or the Madeleine? Or didn't you
get any more postcards?''

"No," thundered the Perelmans so loud that Miss Williams
dropped the Sealyham. "It's all about Americans in Paris. Americans who roll in from the Dome at dawn to find their franc notes
have turned to confetti. Hope Williams is trying to decide between
her job and Fred Keating. The Admiral is miffed because we won't
put a French sailor in the barroom scene for sentimental reasons, and
Eric Dressler is full of vodka and communistic notions. Mary
Phillips? She's walking a high wire between vin et l'eau and a
male dressmaker who lisps. How's that for suspense? We had a
scene at the tomb of Napoleon, but Arthur Sircom talked us out
of it. Said he had a dash of Russian in him and that it always
reminded him of Austerlitz.''

Perelman Tries a Series for TV
Murray Schumach / 1962

The New York Times, 1 March 1962. Copyright © 1962 by The
New York Times Company. Reprinted by permission.

S. J. Perelman, whose search for humor has led him to strange
places and fantastic ideas, talked today of his debut in the curious
world of the television series.

"There was enthusiasm among some people that my book *Acres
and Pains* could be made into a television series," he said. "I
relied on their judgement."

The book is a series of magazine pieces describing the tribulations
of a city person trying to find the alleged joys of life in the country.

"I must confess," said Mr. Perelman, "that I was not a complete
innocent in the world of television. I had been soiled, so to speak,
already. I had done a few single shots for television, but nothing for
a series."

The first step in preparing the pilot for the series—it is now at the
offices of the Columbia Broadcasting System—was the phase
known as the story conference, a sort of children's hour for well-
paid adults.

"I must explain," said Mr. Perelman, "that I had nothing to do
with the writing of the script for the pilot. I had no intention of
revolutionizing the subhuman industry. I was interested in making
the visual kopek or zloty.

"At these story conferences I was acting in the status of supervisor," he continued with mock gravity. "I recall that whenever I
talked about story ideas there was a great deal of buffing at finger-
nails. I assumed they were overworked and sleepy."

The casting of Anne Jackson and Walter Matthau in the leads did
not involve Mr. Perelman. But he was pleased that good actors
had been hired instead of comics. He said he could not explain this
perspicacity on the part of the executives.

Mr. Perelman also had some interesting times during his next
operations in the birth of a television series.

6

"At times, while reading scripts, I reacted with nausea. Yes, I showed this reaction. But only to executives, not to the writers. Pretty sneaky, I suppose. Heads wagged, everyone agreed profoundly. I suppose I made some impression because the next rewrite was different. So was the writer.

"I don't know how they will allocate writing credits on this show. I think the Supreme Court may have to sit on the case. But I was not entirely surprised at this writing procedure. After all, I wrote movie scripts here during the thirties. They used the same system.

Mr. Perelman next found himself on a set at the United Artists-Ziv Studio where the show was being filmed.

"I looked appealing and helpless. The way a writer is supposed to look on a Hollywood set. The only evidence of frenzy during the shooting was when I tripped over a cable and was nearly run down by a hand truck."

The humorist does not know what the show will be titled—assuming that C.B.S. can find sponsors.

"It was my original impression that there was some interest in keeping the title of the book. But it will probably be something like *Meg and Jack* or *Redondo Boulevard*."

Talk with the Author

Newsweek / 1963

Newsweek, 1 July 1963: 58–59. © 1963, Newsweek, Inc. All rights reserved. Reprinted by permission.

The Beauty Part began one day many years ago when S. J. Perelman was riding in the elevator in the Hotel Sutton: Between floors, the operator suddenly announced: "I'm having trouble with my second act."

Perelman shuddered and went home to write about it. Not only does every elevator man have a play, he realized, but as Bert Lahr says in the current play, "every housewife has a novel under her apron."

"It's a cultural upsurge," Perelman said last week, "the big move on the part of everyone for expression. Today everyone is painting, sculpting, dancing. I have a dentist whose walls are filled with his paintings. Mainly my resistance is to those people who imagine they're professional. I object to people who carry music rolls around to be mistaken for music students at Carnegie Hall."

This fooling in the arts is actually an old phenomenon, said Perelman, and begins when parents force talent into children. "I can remember as a kid in Rhode Island doing a Chaplin imitation. A cane, a mustache, baggy trousers. I was purple with shame."

Perelman concocted a series of *New Yorker* stories about this cultural explosion and from the stories he wove *The Beauty Part.* The title has to do with the good that comes with the bad. Perelman explains: "People say, 'My uncle got a job in a cafeteria. He has to work all night, but the beauty part is he can bring home stale Danish pastry'."

The Beauty Part was tried out the summer before last, and again on the road the past four weeks. Did the author have to make changes at the behest of the producer? "Mr. Behest, the producer, chewing on his cigar," said Perelman, chewing on his cigarette, "takes one look at the show, and says, 'It won't work, honey.' His niece from Nebbish, N.D., takes one look and she tells him what's wrong with it. 'Good try. Needs work,' says the producer and the playwright retires to his midnight chicken sandwich and tries to rewrite."

Neither Mr. Behest nor his niece bothered Perelman on *The Beauty Part*. But he still went through many midnight chickens before he came up with the current script. The beauty part, for Perelman, was no matter how much he tinkered, he himself would never have to face an audience. "A playwright is like a tailor," he said. "He has to fit the pants to a man who will stand in front of a triple mirror. The actor has to get up and withstand the scorn."

Standing in for Perelman in front of the mirror is his friend Bert Lahr. "The last of the great clowns," says Perelman. "Perelman's a magician with the English language," says Lahr.

Perelman has expressed his magic in essays, stories, plays, and movies. One medium has eluded him—the comic novel. He doesn't miss it. "I don't think the work of a mural painter has any more worth than that of a miniaturist."

What's next for the miniaturist Perelman? "I may fling the feather pen as far as it goes and get back to what matters," he said, then paused, and clarified, "by which I mean, drinking and wenching."

Travel Talk

Robert S. Kane / 1963

Playbill 25 February 1963. PLAYBILL ® is a registered trademark of PLAYBILL, Incorporated, New York, NY.

It was a near-zero afternoon. S. J. Perelman was warming himself with coffee in the bar-lounge of a Manhattan hotel. He had obtained the beverage with great difficulty from a surly waiter who resented his not ordering stronger stuff. "That man," observed Mr. Perelman, peering without malice through the tiny lenses of Dickensian steel-rimmed spectacles, "has just graduated *cum laude* from a Seminar in Rudeness."

Mr. Perelman was taking a respite from preparing for a four-month round-the-planet writing trip which was about to commence with a New York-Southampton journey on Cunard's great lady, the *Queen Elizabeth*. His current Broadway comedy, *The Beauty Part,* had kept him occupied on home ground for nearly two years. "My dream," he said—again without malice—"is to get as far away from actors as I can. But I shall probably be put at a shipboard table with an itinerant band of Shakespearians traveling, as I shall be, from Mombasa to the Seychelles." The Perelman itinerary, it can be seen, does not constitute a Grand Tour in the ordinary sense.

There will be a return to Africa (Mr. Perelman's first visit there was as impartial observer on an all-girl safari). From the Kenyan port of Mombasa, the small, trim, moustachioed man—who writes his name in large white letters across each piece of luggage, to make for instant identification at customs, journeys by steamer to the British island-colony of the Seychelles. India then, with a tiger-shoot the prelude to an interlude in the Shan States of Burma. Pnom-Penh, the Cambodian capital, and the still-dazzling ruins of Angkor will follow. Then will come the Indonesian jewel of Bali, a tour of Japan, and New York via Europe.

Mr. Perelman, who has visited every continent save South

America and Australia, travels with gusto but without delusions.
For example:

> "All travel—except possibly journeys into space, which do not tempt
> me—is conditioned by one's laundry. At the sight of soiled shirts
> bubbling out of the edges of your suitcase, you are forced to stop, like it
> or not."

> "Hotel concierges must be approached realistically. I sometimes suspect
> that there are among them members of a band of philatelist-brigands who
> amass great collections of stamps unlicked from innocently-penned post-
> cards."

> "The visa-inoculation orgy is calculated to raise the blood pressure and
> harden the arteries. I recall collapsing on a Berlitz classroom floor on
> a day several years ago—prior to a Far Eastern trip—just after my veins
> were filled with typhoid serum, while I was being taught the Malay for
> 'The chicken is on the blackboard.' "

> "Bon Voyage gifts can be dangerous. In the old days, we lost our
> precious travel documents individually. Now, we're given passport
> cases in which we can fit them all—and lose the lot in one fell swoop."

> "Timing is everything, and not only in the theatre. I shall not forget a
> flight some years back. We were served an elaborate lunch and hit an
> air pocket just after digesting it, at which time two electric signs were
> instantly illuminated: 'Fasten Seat Belts' and 'Restroom Occupied.' "

Is it all worth it? "By all means. My ambition is to live out of a
paper suitcase in the Dixie Hotel—and take off at will. Our lives
seem to become so solidly permanent that the transient in us
rarely surfaces."

S. J. Perelman

William Cole and George Plimpton / 1963

S. J. Perelman has an eighty-acre farm in Bucks County, Pennsylvania (where the house is "shingled with second-hand wattles"), a Greenwich Village apartment, and a no-nonsense, one-room office, also in the Village. It was there that the interview took place. The office is furnished like a slightly luxurian monk's cell: a few simple chairs, a desk, a cot. On the walls are a Stuart Davis water color and photographs of James Joyce, Somerset Maugham, and the late Gus Lobrano, a New Yorker editor and close friend of the author. The only bizarre touch is David Niven's hat from *Around the World in 80 Days,* mounted on a pedestal.

Mr. Perelman, trim and well-tailored, is of medium build. His hair is gently receding, and graying at the temples. He wears old-fashioned steel-rimmed spectacles, bought in Paris many years ago. He is soft-spoken and reserved, sometimes chilling, and gives the impression that he does not suffer "nudniks" gladly. He cares about words in their proper places; in his speech each sentence emerges whole and well-balanced, and each generally contains one or two typically Perelmanesque words. He is impatient with obvious questions—those that he has been asked over and over again in hundreds of interviews—but lights up when talking about his days in Hollywood, or telling anecdotes about his friend Robert Benchley. As *The Listener* put it, reporting on a television interview, "Mr. Perelman knew all the answers and gave such as he chose."

Interviewer: We've always been intrigued that when your first book, *Dawn Ginsbergh's Revenge,* appeared in '29, there was no author's name on the title page. Why?

Perelman: Well, it was really an oversight of my own. I was so exalted at being collected for the first time that, in correcting the galleys, I completely overlooked the fact that there was no author's name on the title page. Unless one happened to look at the spine of the book, there would be every implication that it was written by its publisher, Horace Liveright.

Interviewer: Do you look back on your work with pleasure? How long is it since you've re-examined *Dawn Ginsbergh's Revenge*?

Perelman: I haven't actually looked on it for some time. As far as deriving any pleasure, it would be quite the reverse.

Interviewer: Is that true of all your pieces?

Perelman: Well, there are a couple of them I consider verbal zircons if not gems. In *Raymond Chandler Speaking,* a recently-published collection of his letters, I ran across a very flattering reference he made to a parody of his work I had done, "Farewell, My Lovely Appetizer." So I reread a few pages of that to see whether the praise was merited. I prefer not to say whether I think so or not. Otherwise, let me assure you I don't sit in the chimney corner cackling over what I've written.

Interviewer: Is that because of the effort you put into each piece?

Perelman: Possibly. I very much doubt whether I work harder than any other writer, but this particular kind of sludge is droned over while working so that it becomes incantatory and quite sickening for me, at least, to reread.

Interviewer: So much of it is pure art and skill, I should think one would say, "My God, how did I make that association, that connection?"

Perelman: I don't know whether I approve of the picture you suggest of me, lounging about admiring myself in a hand mirror.

Interviewer: Well, in those rare instances when you reread something after a few years, do you get the feeling you should have done something else to a sentence, to a phrase?

Perelman: No, I generally feel astonished at whatever I put down in the first place. The effort of writing seems more arduous all the time. Unlike technicians who are supposed to become more proficient with practice, I find I've grown considerably less articulate.

Interviewer: Is that because you are increasingly more selective?

Perelman: Could be. Also the variety of subjects is restricted the longer I stay at this dodge.

Interviewer: Why?

Perelman: Well, principally through sheer ennui on my part. I've sought material, for example, in the novels I read in my youth, the movies I saw, my Hollywood years, and in advertising. Ultimately, I began to regard these matters as boring. I always grieve for the poor souls who have to grind out a daily humorous column or a weekly piece—people like H. I. Phillips who are obligated to be comical on whatever topic. I remember Benchley did a column three times a week at one time and ran into deep trouble. It's just not possible, in my view.

Interviewer: There were more of those columns back in the twenties and thirties when Don Marquis was working that way, and F.P.A.

Perelman: Well, Marquis fortunately had Archie, his cockroach, and the Old Soak. When you create character it's much easier, because you can keep that spinning. In Frank Adams's case, let's not overlook the extensive help he got from contributors—Ira Gershwin, Sam Hoffenstein, Arthur Kober, Yip Harburg—a pretty respectable roster of names.

Interviewer: In the introduction to *The Most of S. J. Perelman* Dorothy Parker referred to you as a "humorist writer." Do you think of yourself as a humorist writer?

Perelman: I may be doing Mrs. Parker an injustice, but I think the linotyper had one drink too many, and that "humorous" was what was intended. In my more pompous moments I like to think of myself as a writer rather than a humorist, but I suppose that's merely the vanity of advancing age.

Interviewer: Mrs. Parker has said that there aren't any humorists any more . . . except for Perelman. She went on to say, "There's no need for them. Perelman must be very lonely." Are there humorists? Is there a need for them, and are you lonely?

Perelman: Well, it must be thoroughly apparent how many more people wrote humor for the printed page in the twenties. The form seems to be passing, and there aren't many practitioners left. The only magazine nowadays that carries any humor worthy of the name, in my estimation, is *The New Yorker*. Thirty years ago, on the other hand, there were *Judge, Life, Vanity Fair, College Humor*, and one or two others. I think the explanation for the paucity of written humor is simply that very few fledgling writers deign to bother with it. If someone has a flair for comedy, he usually goes into television or what remains of motion pictures. There's far more loot in those fields, and while it's ignominious to be an anonymous gagman, perhaps, eleven hundred dollars a week can be very emollient to the ego. The life of the free-lance writer of humor is highly speculative and not to be recommended as a vocation. In the technical sense, the comic writer is a cat on a hot tin roof. His invitation to perform is liable to wear out at any moment; he must quickly and constantly amuse in a short span, and the first smothered yawn is a signal to get lost. The fiction writer, in contrast, has much more latitude. He's allowed to side-slip into exposition, to wander off into interminable byways and browse around endlessly in his characters' heads. The development of a comic idea has to be swift and economical; consequently, the pieces are shorter than conventional fiction and fetch a much smaller stipend.

Interviewer: Is this the reason so few comic novels are written?

Perelman: Well, the comic novel, I feel, is perhaps the most difficult form a writer can attempt. I can think of only three or four successful ones—*Cakes and Ale, Count Bruga,* and *Lucky Jim. Zuleika Dobson* is often held forth, but the sad fact is that it falls apart two-thirds of the way through, ending rather lamely with the mass suicide at Oxford.

Interviewer: Would you call *The Ginger Man* a comic novel?

Perelman: Rather terrifying. I think it's funny in spots, but many people boggle at certain scabrous passages early in the book. In a way, it's a pity the author should have retained them, because they add little and, on the whole, constrict the fun. . . . The name of F. Anstey, rarely heard nowadays, deserves honorable mention when comic novels are discussed. He edited *Punch* in the late nineties and was also a very successful playwright. He worked for the most part in the realm of fantasy and turned out some very diverting stories—*Vice Versa, The Brass Bottle,* and specifically *The Tinted Venus,* which Ogden Nash and I used as the basis for a musical we wrote called *One Touch of Venus.*

Interviewer: Was Anstey an influence on you? Would you talk a little about your admirations?

Perelman: I stole from the very best sources. I was, and still remain, a great admirer of George Ade, who flourished in this country between 1905 and 1915, and who wrote a good many fables in slang that enjoyed a vogue in my youth. I was also a devotee of Stephen Leacock and, of course, Ring Lardner, who at his best was the nonpareil; nobody in America has ever equaled him. One day, I hope, some bearded Ph.D. will get around—belatedly—to tracing the indebtedness of John O'Hara and a couple other of my colleagues to Lardner. In addition to Ade, Leacock, and Lardner, I was also an earnest student of Benchley, Donald Ogden Stewart, and Frank Sullivan—and we mustn't forget Mencken. At the time I was being forcefully educated, in the early twenties, Mencken and Nathan had a considerable impact, and many of us undergraduates modeled our prose styles on theirs.

Interviewer: How would you describe the form you work in? You've called it "the sportive essay" in a previous interview.

Perelman: I classify myself as a writer of what the French call *feuilletons*—that is, a writer of little leaves. They're comic essays of a particular type.

Interviewer: Are there any devices you use to get yourself going on them?

Perelman: No, I don't think so. Just anguish. Just sitting and staring at the typewriter and avoiding the issue as long as possible. Raymond Chandler and I discussed this once, and he admitted to the most bitter reluctance to commit anything to paper. He evolved the following scheme: he had a tape recorder into which he spoke the utmost nonsense—a stream of consciousness which was then transcribed by a secretary and which he then used as a basis for his first rough draft. Very laborious. He strongly advised me to do the same . . . in fact became so excited that he kept plying me with information for months about the machine that helped him.

Interviewer: Hervey Allen, the author of *Anthony Adverse,* apparently had the voices of his ancestors to help him. All he had to do was lie on a bed, close his eyes, and they went to work for him.

Perelman: I fully believe it, judging from my memory of his work.

Interviewer: How many drafts of a story do you do?

Perelman: Thirty-seven. I once tried doing thirty-three, but something was lacking, a certain—how shall I say?—*je ne sais quoi.* On another occasion, I tried forty-two versions, but the final effect was too lapidary—you know what I mean, Jack? What the hell are you trying to extort—my trade secrets?

Interviewer: . . . merely to get some clue to the way you work.

Perelman: With the grocer sitting on my shoulder. The only thing that matters is the end product, which must have *brio*—or, as you Italians put it, vivacity.

Interviewer: Speaking of vivacity, you have been quoted as saying that the Walpurgisnacht scene in *Ulysses* is the greatest single comic achievement in the language.

Perelman: I was quoted accurately. And here's something else to quote. Joyce was probably one of the most careful writers who ever lived. I have been studying the work you mentioned for nigh on thirty-five years, and I still choke up with respect.

Interviewer: Your writing—like Joyce's, in fact—presupposes a great deal of arcane knowledge on the part of your reader. There are references to cultural figures and styles long past, obsolete words, architectural oddities—reverberations that not everybody will catch. Do you agree that you're writing for a particularly cultured audience?

Perelman: Well, I don't know if that grocer on my shoulder digs all the references, but other than him, I write pretty much for myself. If, at the close of business each evening, I myself can understand what I've written, I feel the day hasn't been totally wasted.

Interviewer: Perhaps you would talk about the incongruity that turns up so often in your use of language.

Perelman: And then perhaps I would not. Writers who pontificate about their own use of language drive me right up the wall. I've discovered that this is an occupational disease of those ladies with three-barreled names one meets at the Authors' League, the P.E.N. Club, and so forth. In what spare time I have, I read the expert opinions of V. S. Pritchett and Edmund Wilson, who are to my mind the best-qualified authorities on the written English language. Vaporizing about one's own stylistic intricacies strikes me as being visceral, and, to be blunt, inexcusable.

Interviewer: In your own writing, when you're at work, thinking hard, and a particularly felicitous expression or phrase comes to mind, do you laugh?

Perelman: When I was going I used to literally roll over and over on the floor with delight, marveling at the intricacy of the mind that had wrought such gems. I've become much less supple in late middle age.

Interviewer: It's often said—or taught, anyway—that what seems at first blush funny is usually not. Would that be a good maxim in writing humor?

Perelman: In writing anything, sweetie. The old apothegm that easy writing makes hard reading is as succinct as ever. I used to know several eminent writers who were given to boasting of the speed with which they created. It's not a lovable attribute, to put it mildly, and I'm afraid our acquaintanceship has languished.

Interviewer: The country's comics can't write a book or even a piece of any value at all. Why is that?

Perelman: You're confusing comedians—that is to say, performers—with writers. The two have entirely different orientations. How many writers do you know who can run around a musical-comedy stage like Groucho Marx, or, for that matter, talk collectedly into a microphone? Only a genius like David Susskind can do everything.

Interviewer: I'd like to ask about the frequent use of Yiddish references and expressions throughout your writing. Words like "nudnik" and "schlepp" and "tzimmas" come in frequently enough.

Perelman: Your pronunciation of "nudnik," by the way, is appalling. It's "nudnik," not "noodnik." As to why I occasionally use the words you indicate, I like them for their invective content. There are nineteen words in Yiddish that convey gradations of disparagement from a mild, fluttery helplessness to a state of downright, irreconcilable brutishness. All of them can be usefully employed to pin-point the kind of individuals I write about.

Interviewer: Almost all the humorous writers of your period have worked in Hollywood. How do you look back on the time you served there?

Perelman: With revulsion. I worked there sporadically from 1931 to 1942, and I can say in all sincerity that I would have spent my time to better advantage on Tristan da Cunha.

Interviewer: Does that include your association with the Marx

Brothers, for whom you worked on *Monkey Business* and *Horse Feathers?*

Perelman: I've dealt exhaustively with this particular phase of my life: to such a degree, in fact, that the mere mention of Hollywood induces a condition in me like breakbone fever. It was a hideous and untenable place when I dwelt there, populated with few exceptions by Yahoos, and now that it has become the chief citadel of television, it's unspeakable. Could we segue into some other subject?

Interviewer: Yes, but before we do, might we stimulate your memory of any colleagues of yours—writers humorous or otherwise—who functioned in Hollywood during the time you spent there?

Perelman: Well, of course everyone imaginable worked there at one time or another, and the closest analogy I can draw to describe the place is that it strikingly resembled the Sargasso Sea—an immense, turgidly revolving whirlpool in which literary hulks encrusted with verdigris moldered until they sank. It was really quite startling, at those buffet dinners in Beverly Hills, to encounter some dramatist or short-story writer out of your boyhood, or some one-shot lady novelist who'd had a flash success, who was now grinding out screenplays about the Cisco Kid for Sol Wurtzel. I remember, one day on the back lot at M-G-M, that a pallid wraith of a man erupted from a row of ramshackle dressing rooms and embraced me as though we had encountered each other in the Empty Quarter of Arabia. He was a geezer I'd known twelve years before on *Judge* magazine, a fellow who ran some inconsequential column full of Prohibition jokes. When I asked him what he was doing, he replied that he had been writing a screenplay of "Edwin Drood" for the past two years. He confessed quite candidly that he hadn't been able as yet to devise a finish, which, of course, wasn't too surprising inasmuch as Charles Dickens couldn't do so either.

Interviewer: Surely you must have drawn some comfort from the presence of writers like Robert Benchley, Dorothy Parker, and Donald Ogden Stewart?

Perelman: It goes without saying, but since you've said it, I can only agree most emphatically. You happen to have mentioned a remarkable trio, all of them people who had no more connection

with the screen-writing fraternity than if they'd been Martians.
Benchley and Mrs. Parker differed from Stewart in the sense that
neither of them ever made an accommodation with Hollywood.
Stewart did; he was a highly paid screenwriter for many years,
made a great deal of loot there, and managed to get it out. The
last is quite a trick, because that fairy money they paid you had a
way of evaporating as you headed east through the Cajon Press.
But whereas Stewart was a consecrated scenarist, Mrs. Parker and
Benchley viewed Hollywood with utter accuracy, is my belief.

Interviewer: Which was what?

Perelman: As a dreary industrial town controlled by hoodlums of
enormous wealth, the ethical sense of a pack of jackals, and taste
so degraded that it befouled everything it touched. I don't mean to
sound like a boy Savonarola, but there were times, when I drove
along the Sunset Strip and looked at those buildings, or when I
watched the fashionable film colony arriving at some premiere at
Grauman's Egyptian, that I fully expected God in his wrath to
obliterate the whole shebang. It was—if you'll allow me to use a
hopelessly inexpressive word—*dégoutant*.

Interviewer: Feeling as you assert Mrs. Parker and Mr. Benchley
did, and as you plainly did, how could you manage to remain
there for even limited periods?

Perelman: We used to ask each other that with great frequency.
The answer, of course, was geetus—gelt—scratch. We all badly
needed the universal lubricant, we all had dependents and insurance
policies and medical bills, and the characters who ran the celluloid
factories were willing to lay it on the line. After all, it was no worse
than playing the piano in a whorehouse.

Interviewer: Do you feel that Hollywood evolved any writers of
consequence, men and women who did important and memorable
work in the medium?

Perelman: Oh, certainly—Frances Goodrich and Albert Hackett,
Robert Riskin, and one or two others—but actually, it was a
director's medium rather than a writer's. Men like W. S. Van Dyke;
Frank Capra, George Cukor, Mitchell Leisen, William Wyler, and
John Huston were the real film-makers, just as their predecessors in
the silent era had been. I always felt that the statement attributed
to Irving Thalberg, the patron saint at Metro-Goldwyn-Mayer,

beautifully summed up the situation: "The writer is a necessary evil." As a sometime employee of his, I consider that a misquotation. I suspect he said "weevil."

Interviewer: Haven't there been writers who originated in films and then went on to make a contribution on Broadway?

Perelman: Well, after scratching my woolly poll for half an hour, I can think of three—Dore Schary, Norman Krasna, and Leonard Spigelgass—but I believe I am in my legal rights in refusing to assess their contribution. We shall have to leave that to the verdict of history, and meanwhile permit me to soothe my agitated stomach with this Gelusil tablet.

Interviewer: Do you ever revisit Hollywood?

Perelman: Every few years, and never out of choice. The place has become pretty tawdry by now; there was a time, back in the early thirties, when all the stucco and the Georgian shop fronts were fresh, and, while the architecture was hair-raising, there was enough greenery to soften it. But they've let the place go down nowadays—Hollywood proper is cracked and crazed, the gilt's peeling, and the whole thing has a depressing bargain-basement air. Beverly Hills, except for a few streets, is a nightmare; the entrance to it, which used to be a field of poinsettias, now sports a bank that must be the single most horrendous structure in the world. Of course, I except the Guggenheim Museum on Fifth Avenue.

Interviewer: In short, then, you experience almost no feelings of nostalgia when you return to Southern California?

Perelman: Sir, you are a matter of understatement.

Interviewer: Nathanael West lived in Hollywood, and wrote a remarkable book about it, *The Day of the Locust*. He was your brother-in-law. And you are his literary executor?

Perelman: Whatever that implies. In any case it takes the form of being the recipient of a lot of slush mail from ambitious people working toward a degree, usually a doctorate. The curious thing is that every single one of them nurses the delusion that he has discovered Nathanael West, and that with his thesis West will receive the recognition he's entitled to. It keeps the incinerator going full time.

Interviewer: You knew F. Scott Fitzgerald in Hollywood?

Perelman: Yes—in a period of his life that must have been one of his most trying. The anxieties and pressures of his private life, combined with the decline of his reputation, had nearly overwhelmed him, and he was seeking to re-establish himself as a writer for films. He didn't succeed, and I don't believe he ever would have. He was pathetically innocent about the kind of hypocrisy and the infighting one had to practice to exist in the industry.

Interviewer: Did you ever see Faulkner out there?

Perelman: Very infrequently. Sometimes, of a Sunday morning, he used to stroll by a house I occupied in Beverly Hills. I noticed him only because the sight of anybody walking in that environment stamped him as an eccentric, and indeed, it eventually got him into trouble. A prowl car picked him up and he had a rather sticky time of it. The police were convinced he was a finger man for some jewelry mob planning to knock over one of the fancy residences.

Interviewer: Your reluctance to discuss Hollywood is so manifest that we will change the venue to a more metropolitan one. *The New Yorker* is known as the most closely edited magazine of all time. What can you tell us of its interior structure?

Perelman: No more than you would have gleaned from Thurber's disquisitions on the subject. Personally, I thought that in *The Years with Ross* he made the paper and its staff sound prankish, like a bunch of schoolboys playing at journalism. But one must remember that Thurber's entire life was bound up in *The New Yorker* and that on occasion he was inclined to deify it. At a gathering one evening during the mid-thirties, when he was extolling its glories and parenthetically his major share in creating them, I mildly suggested that a sense of moderation was indicated and that it was merely another fifteen-cent magazine. Thurber sprang on me, and, had it not been for the intercession of several other contributors, unquestionably would have garrotted me.

Interviewer: How often did Ross or *The New Yorker* come up with an idea or a suggestion for a piece?

Perelman: Not too often. Most of the suggestions I get originate in mysterious quarters. They drift in from kindly readers, or I spot something—

Interviewer: There are kindly readers?

Perelman: There are, and I'm continually heartened by the fact that people take the time to forward a clipping or a circular they feel might inspire me.

Interviewer: Does it worry you, since you often pick very contemporary subjects to write about, that your work may become outdated?

Perelman: Sir, the answer to that is that I regard myself as a species of journalist, and that questions of imperishability are at best idle. At my most euphoric, I don't expect to outlast Mount Rushmore.

Interviewer: Have you ever considered a serious book?

Perelman: It may surprise you to hear me say—and I'll thank you not to confuse me with masters of the paradox like Oscar Wilde and G. K. Chesterton—that I regard my comic writing as serious. For the past thirty-four years, I have been approached almost hourly by damp people with foreheads like Rocky Ford melons who urge me to knock off my frivolous career and get started on that novel I'm burning to write. I have no earthly intention of doing any such thing. I don't believe in the importance of scale; to me the muralist is no more valid than the miniature painter. In this very large country, where size is all and where Thomas Wolfe outranks Robert Benchley, I am content to stitch away at my embroidery hoop. I think the form I work can have its own distinction, and I would like to surpass what I have done in it.

Groucho, Perelman, and Tynan Talk about Funny Men

Kenneth Tynan / 1964

From *The Observer*, 14 June 1964. Reprinted by permission.

More than 30 years have passed since Groucho Marx and S. J. Perelman first worked together. According to myth, the classic early quartet of Marx Brothers pictures (*Horse Feathers, Monkey Business, Duck Soup* and *Animal Crackers?*) was written single-handed by Perelman; in fact he wrote only the first two, and gets embarrassed when people hail him as the sole literary progenitor of the Brothers and their legend. He saw Groucho in a Broadway show in the late twenties and sent a fervent note backstage; the result was an invitation to Hollywood and a friendship that has survived repeated allegations that Groucho owes everything to Perelman and vice versa.

I met them for lunch at the Connaught Hotel. Side by side, when I entered the lobby, sat two middle-aged men with plenty of head visible through their hair. Both wore tweed suits and striped shirts with button-down collars. Both had toothbrush moustaches, of which Perelman's was straw-coloured and upswept, while Groucho's was close-cropped and grey. At 60, Perelman is Groucho's junior by nine years and you notice at once that he defers to his elder as a performer. Similarly, Groucho defers to Perelman as an intellectual. They are both New Yorkers and Jewish; Perelman was born in Brooklyn and Groucho on Manhattan upper East Side.

We move to the restaurant, Groucho leading the way in his low-slung, loping gait (a shell-less tortoise turned biped?), with Perelman in jaunty pursuit. Over Vichysoisse we talk about Jewishness and its enormous formative influence on show business in the United States. Harry Kurnitz, a Hollywood wit respected by both my guests, once went to a crowded theatrical restaurant in Manhattan with a friend who said: "Do you realise, Harry, that there

are two million Jews in New York alone?'' Kurnitz looked around
him and replied: ''What do you mean—alone?'' Why is it that the best
comedians are so often Jewish—Eddie Cantor, Phil Silvers, Sid
Caesar, Danny Kaye, Jack Benny, Mort Sahl, Lenny Bruce,
George Burns, Milton Berle, Bert Lahr, the Marxes, etc.?

''I think it's because the Jews were immigrants,'' says Perelman,
''They were wrestling with English as a foreign language. They'd take
an Anglo-Saxon cliché—like 'I disbursed a goodly sum'—and make
it funny by pronouncing it in the wrong accent.'' In other words,
pedantry and polysyllables become comic when uttered by Jews.

Groucho dissents. ''You taught me that,'' he says askance to
Perelman, ''but then I was trying to be an intellectual.'' (He says
nearly everything askance.) Groucho doesn't think Jewishness is
the vital factor in American comedy; he attributes the Jewish
hegemony to the fact that most American comedy is urban, and that
most big cities have a large Jewish population.

Many Marx Brothers fans, especially in the early days, refused
to believe that Groucho, Chico and Harpo were related to one
another. Others insisted that they were a bunch of Italians. American slang for Italian is ''Ginnie'' (pronounced ''guinea''), and
Groucho recalls a description he overheard in a theatre lobby of
himself and his brothers: ''One's a Ginnie, one's a Jew and the
other spits on the sidewalk.'' Longevity, he thinks, is the quality
that makes Jewish performers unique, and he ascribes it to
something unconnected with talent: ''It's because Jews don't drink.
Or at least, not much. Whenever Jewish comics get together, the bar
bill is small. You can imagine how dull our New Years are.'' During
lunch he drank nothing but water.

Prompted by Perelman, he recalls an occasion when George
Burns (the comedian and former partner of Gracie Allen) was
touring in vaudeville with a Jewish girl disguised as a Spanish
dancer. In the course of the act she would twirl at his fingertips,
revealing as she did so a pair of bushily unshaven armpits. After
their opening night, the manager called Burns to one side. ''I like
your act,'' he said, ''but I don't like those two Jews you're dancing
with.''

Perelman blames TV for having extinguished the racial (e.g.,
Jewish) comic: because the sponsors are scared to offend minori-

ties, comedy that has its roots in a particular racial or national idiom tends to get ironed out into anonymity. I ask where it is possible nowadays for a young comic to learn his trade before a live audience as Groucho and his brothers so rigorously did.

"There's no vaudeville now," Groucho says, "so it's tough. The main outlet is clubs—small nightspots in places like Cincinnati or Waco, Texas. The big difference is that there used to be 'action comics' like me and my brothers. But there's no room for that kind of group comedy on the television screen. So today you get mostly stand-up comics—one man with a microphone." Perelman adds: "They're all monologuists now."

Both eat frugally: pressed beef for Perelman and a ham omelette for Groucho. "It's 30 years since my brothers and I made our English debut," says Groucho. "It was a disaster. The audience threw copper coins on to the stage of the Coliseum. I walked down to the footlights and told them to throw silver, preferably wrapped in bank-notes." Decades of affluence have not banished the spectre of poverty. Groucho sympathises with the Left and disapproves of the monarchy ("Why should they live off the people?"); but age has sweetened his attitude towards capitalism. "I've got to the stage," he admits, "where I read the *Wall Street Journal* before I read *Variety*."

"What are you hawking there?" he bawls suavely at the waiter with the sweet trolley, and orders a fruit salad. Coffee precipitates more reminiscence. Perelman tells me with moist eyes about the West Side Writing and Asthma Club which he and Groucho founded in the thirties. Levy's Tavern on Ninth Street was its headquarters, and the guests who attended its daily lunches included Robert Benchley, Donald Ogden Stewart, the actor Charles Butterworth, and the notoriously eccentric song-writers Bert Kalmar and Harry Ruby (authors of "Show me a rose—I'll show you a stag at bay").

Groucho, still at large in memory lane, comes up with an account of the most extraordinary vaudeville act he ever saw. It was called *Swain's Rats and Cats*, and it consisted of rats dressed up as jockeys and cats dressed up as horses. Every night they raced around a miniature track. One evening Fanny Brice, a Ziegfeld star who was topping the bill, went into her dressing-room and en-

countered one of Swain's rats stark naked (the rat, not Miss Brice).
She screamed, whereupon the rat was seized and reprimanded.
Next week it appeared at the Palace in New York and won every
race. The critics congratulated Swain on his new, world-beating
rat. "Not at all," he said proudly. "This is a rat who has been in
Fanny Brice's dressing-room. This is a self-made rat." Of Miss
Brice herself, Groucho remembers that "her language was that of
Pier Six, and she always carried five sets of teeth—including one
for signing autographs in and another for just walking down the
street."

I ask him to name the people who have made him laugh. "The
funniest talkers," he says, "the funniest men around a dinner-
table would be George Jessel and George Burns. The fastest men
with one-line gags would be Oscar Levant and George S. Kaufman. On stage, I would pick W. C. Fields, Willie Howard, Ed
Wynn, Bobby Clark and Bert Lahr. But it's hard to laugh at
comedians if you're a comedian, especially if they're getting
laughs." Perelman's list of great comics is the same, except that it
includes Groucho.

When we parted, Perelman was Balkan-bound. What of Groucho?
Well, he won't appear at Las Vegas ("I don't want to work for
hoodlums and gangsters"), but he might take part in an American
TV series, playing a dead grandpa who makes ghostly intrusions
into the life of a married couple. His immediate commitment, when
the taxi engulfed him last weekend, was to snatch some sleep before
dining with T. S. Eliot. Eliot wrote to him several years ago asking
for an autographed picture. He sent one, feeling greatly honoured;
but Eliot replied insisting on another, in which his cigar was tilted
at a more challenging angle. Groucho complied, and was forthwith
invited to dinner. What happened when they met I do not know,
but there are plenty of Eliot lyrics that would suit the vinegary
wryness of Groucho's singing voice to perfection. I should love to
hear his recording of "Under the bam, under the boo"—and
what about:—

> "I'll carry you off
> To a cannibal isle . . .
>   Yes, I'd eat you!
> In a nice little, white little, soft little, tender little,
> Juicy little, right little missionary stew"?

Groucho is the ideal vocal stand-in for Sweeney Agonistes. And if Eliot were contemplating an EP release of "O O O O that Shakespeherian Rag," he could not have chosen an apter year, or a better minstrel.

Conversations

Roy Newquist / 1967

From *Conversations* by Roy Newquist. Rand McNally, 1967:275–86.

"Humor in its simplest form, is the unexpected . . . it is the sudden disruption of thought, the conjoining of unlikely elements. It's the nostalgic reference that pleases or delights people."

Perelman: I was born in New York in 1904 and reared in Rhode Island, where I attended Brown University. Simply stated, I became interested in the life creative because I was a comic artist at college. I was more interested in working for the college humor magazine, *The Brown Jug,* than I was in trigonometry and all those necessary adjuncts. Eventually, in my senior year, I became editor of the magazine and subsequently went professional in New York as a comic artist. This lasted for six or seven years, when I drifted into writing, principally because my cartoon captions became longer and longer and longer. Finally, having become somewhat schizophrenic, I decided I'd better become a writer rather than a comic artist. And in 1931 I ran afoul of the Marx Brothers and did a hitch or two for them—*Monkey Business* and *Horse Feathers.*

After that a sortie into the theater. The first show I did was a review for Beatrice Lillie and Bobby Clark titled *Walk a Little Faster.* It didn't move in as spritely a fashion as the title might indicate. It had a very moderate success, indeed, which we all ascribed to the great Depression. Its most notable feature was a song, now famous—"April in Paris." Music by Vernon Duke, lyrics by E. Y. Harburg. Forgive me for sounding like a catalog of names, but we were all neophytes; this was the first Broadway attempt by all of us.

Shortly after I should have walked a little faster I began working

29

for *The New Yorker* and have worked for it rather steadily ever
since, interspersing with bouts on Broadway and in Hollywood.

I started off under Harold Ross, of course. It's difficult to describe
him in light of Jim Thurber's book about him because that book
is so all-enveloping. I don't agree with all of it, but Ross was
actually an inspired man. The magazine was his entire life, and
properly so, because he conceived it originally as a magazine for
metropolitan New York. He started it in 1925, when there was no
such animal, and *The New Yorker* actually displaced a number of
comic magazines that had existed until then, including the old *Life*
magazine, *Judge,* and (prior to both of them) *Puck.* What *The New
Yorker* did was create an urbane and well-edited magazine that
didn't cater to the level of the barbershop mentality. It tried to
appeal to literate people, and it's always been my view that it is
extremely well-edited, civilized, and intelligent. I have great admiration for it.

Nor has *The New Yorker* changed appreciably from the day of
Ross to the present editorship of William Shawn. Some of the
articles have become longer. Whether it's become more serious a
magazine I don't know. I think it was a serious magazine during
the 1930s; it couldn't help but be. After all, the times were so
terribly out of joint. *The New Yorker* has always carried a great
deal of extremely good reportage; the excellence of people like
Janet Flanner and John Hersey goes without saying, and Robert
Chaplain, now reporting on Southeast Asia, has been great. And in
book reviewing men like Edmund Wilson and V. S. Pritchett have the
finest critical minds in the business.

N: What were the advantages of your long association with *The
New Yorker*?

Perelman: I consider myself purely as a contributor, you know. I
have no staff connection, nor has Updike or Cheever or virtually
anyone you can mention. The magazine doesn't have a great mast-
head, like *Time,* where you find literally thousands of names of
editors and subeditors and researchers. (This, to me, is pretentious
behavior.) *The New Yorker* has a small and very efficient staff.
The emphasis is placed entirely on good writing, on clear and
concise lettering. There's a notable lack of phony showmanship.

The personal advantages in working for both Ross and William

Shawn lie in the fact that I've found people who do their best to comprehend what I write, and who give me as much latitude as I can possibly have. I've been able, in the type of writing I do, to go off the deep end if I felt like doing so, yet be condoned and understood. That is enormously important to a writer. I have done considerable work for some of the big, slick, popular magazines, and almost every word I've turned in has been questioned. They seem to feel that certain words are beyond the comprehension of their readers. This seems, to me, a patronizing attitude. I prefer to feel that if I take off at right angles or go off in a flight of fancy, the reader should be given the privilege of being allowed to follow me without being given a crutch by the editor.

N: Are there significant changes in the field of humor that have taken place during your career?

Perelman: You have just handed me a license to pontificate. You see, I consider myself purely traditional, a descendant of people like George Ade, Ring Lardner, Stephen Leacock, Robert Benchley, and Frank Sullivan—people who have worked in the field of free association. That school extends all the way back to the Midwestern humorists, including Twain, who gave us a tradition in humor—at least, of sorts.

What seems to be happening now in the field is a rather dreary emphasis on the sadder aspects of life, less emphasis on what is funny. I suppose it's our reflection of the Depression of the thirties, the World War following that, then the Korean War, and so on. Perhaps young people are no longer interested in doing the sort of free association humor I do; consequently there are very few people plying this particular craft. Yet I'm constantly told that there's a crying need for humor in times as depressing as these, and that people need to laugh. But I don't see many people making the effort. Among newspaper humorists you have Art Buchwald and Russell Baker, both extremely able and talented men. In the magazines there is a remarkable dearth of new people. I can't really account for the lack; perhaps the increasing conformity of American life places real humor at a disadvantage.

You see, a rise in conformity is attended by a decline in eccentricity. I notice this very much. You have only to go to England, for example, to see a country that still nourishes and appreciates her eccentrics. This isn't true here. We're not interested in the eccentric or the old person. Everything is beamed toward youth and spring and bounce, whereas in England the individual who doesn't conform is accepted with some degree of sympathy and rather liked. I don't think that American life condones, much less fosters, eccentricity, and I'm afraid we've descended to a dead level, to a thoroughly uninteresting kind of person who reads certain things, wears certain clothes, drives in certain automobiles, etc. (I shan't mention the sort of thing he reads because I might begin insulting a few periodicals and authors of my acquaintance.)

N: What are the things you find significant in the culture of conformity?

Perelman: I shall start with the theater and work backward. It's no news to anyone that the theater is in a lamentable state in this country. The approaching theatrical season has only three or four plays one would want to go to see, and they're all imports from England. There does seem to be a great deal of vitality and humor in the English theater, but our own native theater seems entirely concerned with transcriptions and reworkings of old material. For example, the new show *Holly Golightly* is only a redo of Capote's *Breakfast at Tiffany's,* and there are at least four or five other shows coming which are variations or adaptations of old material. A strange sort of flaccidity seems to have overtaken our playwrights. And the theater has to start with the playwright. That's where the trouble is. We keep hearing about the lamentable state of health of "the fabulous invalid," and the rascality and venality and homosexuality of the theater, but we've got to start with plays and, in my view, the plays are simply not being written.

As far as books are concerned, we seem to be having an absolute blizzard of ethnic novels about Negroes and Jews. This is all very well, very encouraging to social progress, I presume, but the eyelids tend to droop at the vast number of books written about Jews and Negroes. I can't say what books *should* be written about; if I knew, I'd probably be writing one of them. All I know is that when I go into the bookstore I really have to hold on to a buxom saleslady for support when I see the crop of dreary books on the shelves.

As far as movies (I'm beginning to sound like Jeremiah here), I ask any fair-minded person whether or not the best pictures he's

seen in the last few years haven't been European films. The fact is
that movies as we all knew them during the thirties and forties,
Hollywood at its best, have disappeared. Now all we get out of
Hollywood is something with Rock Hudson and Doris Day, a
tired, dreary stereotype. The best movies come from Italy, Sweden,
France, Poland. All this may be a consequence of the fragmenta-
tion of Hollywood. When the great big studios like Twentieth
Century-Fox and MGM and Paramount fell apart, production
became an individualized matter. Small companies and directors
and writers started joining together to make pictures, but for
some unaccountable reason they chose to imitate the worst features
of the big studio movie instead of picking up the good features. In
recent years pictures have become truly international, and I think
there's been a notable improvement.

During the so-called "Golden Age" in Hollywood, around 1935,
really interesting pictures were produced—*The Thin Man,* the
films of Carole Lombard, the MGM and Paramount specialization
in swift, witty pictures. Then came the best work of people like Billy
Wilder, pictures like *Double Indemnity* which he made with Charles
Brackett. And the early melodramas of James Cagney, like *The
Public Enemy*. They were first-rate. They had vitality and jump and
timeliness. But Hollywood lost out.

N: You worked out there quite a bit. What were your impressions
of the screenwriter's life?

Perelman: I worked out there over a period that can best be
circumscribed as 1931 to 1942, and certainly not all the time. I
went out there from time to time to replenish the larder, and most
of my Hollywood experiences were dismal and unrewarding because the screenwriter in Hollywood (and there were 1,275 of us at
the peak of the movie business!) was subject to all the stress and
strain of supply and demand. He was in the position of a man who
works on a shoe lathe in a place like Lynn, Massachusetts. There
were good times and bad times. Consequently, as a free-lance
screenwriter I was thrown into all sorts of curious ventures.

Once, for example, I worked with Ogden Nash, collaborating on
an attempt to write a screenplay of *How to Win Friends and
Influence People,* which sounds grisly and was, except for the fact
that Nash and I got to know each other well and subsequently

collaborated in the theater on a musical for Mary Martin titled *One Touch of Venus*. We enjoyed doing that; Mary Martin was sublime to work with. But the original screen hitch was a matter of sitting in an office trying to scratch out something for the needs of the producer at that moment. We spent the time profitably at that by inventing a Sherlock Holmes quiz. We did not attend strictly to our knitting.

I also worked on an attempt to do a musical comedy movie based upon a successful British musical, *Nymph Errant*. I was on that for twenty-two weeks, and had three sets of collaborators. The first two sets were gangland experts and spent all their time trying to insert bits about arson and mayhem and violence of all sorts. They were followed by an earnest young radical who kept trying to get social consciousness into the script. This nightmare lasted twenty-two weeks. True, I was getting paid every Wednesday. But the whole film aborted, nothing came of it, and I was left with some of what Dorothy Parker called "fairy money." Hollywood money had a strange way of evaporating. You knew it wasn't real money; unless you spent it fast it had no validity. I used to try to spend it fast by fleeing to Europe, where it seemed to purchase a lot of satisfaction, something it didn't do in Los Angeles.

N: But wasn't your experience with *Around the World in 80 Days* quite satisfying?

Perelman: That was sort of a blood bath too at the time. It brought me into contact with that notable personality, Mike Todd, who was made of the stuff they usually put on the points of fountain pens, iridium, the hardest metal known. Mike did the whole picture, of course, on a shoestring, parlaying his luck throughout, borrowing money left and right, constantly being told by older and wiser heads that the whole thing would be a disaster. I must say that he had a lot of guts. He was a man with an *idée fixee;* he was convinced that *Around the World in 80 Days* was a good property, and he stuck to this project through thick and thin. And it did come out right side up as far as he was concerned.

N: Most of the script was yours, wasn't it?

Perelman: Let's not forget a man named Jules Verne, who thought the whole thing up in the first place. It's awfully hard, when you talk about a screenplay, to tell whose lines are whose. So many situations arise during production when a gaffer or a grip on the set suddenly says to the director, "Hey, wouldn't it be a good idea if she said such-and-such," and they say, "Fine, print it."

In the main I think I can say that a lot of lines were mine, but to chemically assay the whole thing is very difficult. It's a corporate venture, a cooperative venture, you know. It's written or originated by one person, or by fifteen who rewrite each other, and then it's produced in a building the size of an armory with a whole flock of people holding lights and sound booms and moving things. It's distinctly a community project.

N: You mentioned taking your fairy money to Europe. In considering the body of your work I find a great deal concerned with both the pleasures and the vicissitudes of travel. How did your nomadic tendencies come about?

Perelman: I've been going to France with some degree of regularity since 1927. But the first ambitious tour I took was in 1947 when I made a trip around the world with Hirschfeld, the *New York Times* caricaturist, for *Holiday* magazine. That really set me off, and I made a second world tour a few years later, with family intact, and wrote about that in a book titled *Swiss Family Perelman.* (The first was *Westward Ha!*) After all this the vagabond instinct became rooted. I dashed off to East Africa in 1953 and was able to revisit that area a few years ago; since then I've been in Eastern Europe. I really love to travel, and I find, as far as copy is concerned, that the stresses and strains one encounters with customs officials and hotel capers and all that sort of thing is highly productive of the kind of situation I can write about. In other words, misery breeds copy.

N: What is your family status?

Perelman: I was married in 1929 and have two children, a boy and a girl. They're grown up, of course. My base today is Pennsylvania. We have a farm there, a farm we've had since the early thirties. I bought that farm originally with my wife's brother, Nathanael West. West and I had known each other at Brown University, and we remained friends after that, then through the thick and thin of in-law association. West, you know, went into the hotel business in New York, managing a hotel and concurrently writing his first novel, *Miss Lonelyhearts.* Then he drifted out to

Hollywood and lived there for some years while he wrote a succession
of books.

N: You mentioned a fling in theater that actually came quite early
in your career, and then, again, later. Could you single out those
that were the most satisfying?

Perelman: My wife and I wrote a couple of plays together. One
called *All Good Americans* in 1934, a comedy about Americans in
Paris, an expatriate sort of thing. Another, in 1940, titled *The Night
Before Christmas* that dealt with hoodlums who bought a luggage
shop on Sixth Avenue in New York in order to drill into the vault of
a bank adjoining their cellar. Both of these were subsequently
made into movies, and I must say that we had a lot of fun with
both experiences.

I also enjoyed working on the musical I spoke of, *One Touch of
Venus,* with Odgen Nash. Following that I did another musical,
Sweet Bye and Bye, which dealt with the future. I've always thought
about the show in terms of a remark made by Lincoln Steffens,
the great muckraking journalist. When he returned from Russia
after seeing the Russian experiment he was besieged by journalists
who wanted to hear his impressions, and he said, "I've seen the
future and it works." Well, we saw the future, and it didn't work.

The Marx Brothers, earlier in the game, were such jolly good
fellows. Our first experience was the movie *Monkey Business,*
when they were really feeling their way. This was the first thing that
had actually been written for them for the screen. Prior to that
they had made *Coconuts* and *Animal Crackers* as transcriptions
into film from their stage work, but *Monkey Business* was their
first screen original.

Like all first-rate comedians, and I've learned this by working
with other blithe spirits, they were extremely insecure. I think all
comedians are far more insecure than "straight" actors; it seems to
be part and parcel of their natures. They're in constant fret about
whether or not the audience is going to laugh, perhaps because
without laughter the comedian is utterly lost. But at our first point
of contact they were venturing into a world they didn't know at all
well—Hollywood. Consequently, there was no relaxed attitude,
and the writers bore the brunt, so to speak. When that picture was
released and was successful, and we came to work on *Horse*

Feathers, they were much more relaxed because they had more confidence. My particular friend was Groucho, and I've happily been able to remain great friends with him ever since. I have great esteem for Groucho Marx. He has a very quick and civilized mind. However, this shouldn't be news to anyone.

As you probably know, there were originally five Marx Brothers. The fifth, the unknown, was Gummo, who is in the lady's underwear business and has never participated in a theatrical career.

But I do love the theater—the pleasure of working with so many first-rate people, and the response, that immediate response, of the audience.

N: In a different vein, concerning the upcoming writer who would be a writer of humor, what advice would you give him? What would you hope for him?

Perelman: I should think, first of all, that he ought to be an omnivorous reader. He should acquaint himself with everything that's been done. Then, frankly, I would counsel him to be imitative. We hear a great deal, it seems to me, about the necessity for avoiding imitation, but I don't feel that way at all. I feel the young writer has to model himself upon standards they admire, and I base this upon my own experience. I was a slavish admirer of Stephen Leacock and Ring Lardner, and when I now look back upon my early work I find whole chunks that seem to have been lifted out of their works. I think that the more the writer continues and perseveres, the imitative bits tend to drop away. They eventually begin to develop qualities that are idiosyncratic, true to the self, rather apart from the image of whatever hero was in mind.

I do think it is vital to read as much as possible. There is such a great volume of stuff to go on.

As far as opportunities are concerned, I fear that the printed page is going to become less and less valuable. This is an awkward way of saying that the mass communication media are going to take over. Obviously, television and radio have usurped so much of the attention of people that I believed that someone who wants to be a humorous writer is going to have to be thrown into fields like television. I deplore this because the level of most television is so terribly low that I hate to see anyone get involved in the business. I'm sure you've read Merle Miller's very funny book, *Only You, Dick*

Daring, in which the horrors of what a writer in television goes
through are so wonderfully cataloged. But every writer in television
is bound to go through this sort of thing because it is a community
business if ever there was one.

If someone is really, truly devoted to putting words on paper, and
is willing to endure the struggle and make the effort, I would
remind him that there are still some places where his work can be
printed. *The New Yorker* is one of them, and there are some English
magazines, too. Then, of course, some of the smaller magazines,
staid and respectable ones like *Harper's,* occasionally do use
humor.

But the road is rough and the commitment is long.

N: If you were to look back over your own life and career and
pick out those persons who were influential, who would they be?

Perelman: To mention just a few names. The first would be
Robert Benchley, with whom I was fortunate enough to be friends
during a good portion of my career. Dorothy Parker is another
person. Both of these exercised a role in my life which is difficult
to put into words. I had great admiration for both as individuals and
as artists. I think their standards were very high, indeed; and that
just knowing them meant a great deal to me. I'm also sure that
knowing Groucho Marx has meant a great deal. To a lesser degree
there are people like Somerset Maugham and T. S. Eliot, both of
whom I knew. I always had the greatest possible esteem for
Maugham's work and read it from childhood on. Eliot I knew since
1944 or 1945 and saw him frequently in America and in England.
There are also more obscure individuals who exercised a beneficient
effect on my writing and on my personal behavior.

N: We've referred to changes in humor and tastes. I was wonder-
ing if you think public preference has had an effect in supporting
or enforcing changes.

Perelman: I don't know if I'll answer your question directly, but
from the mail I receive as a consequence of what I write, I should say
that people are very alert. I am constantly pleased to find a public
that reads my work, and they do exercise a regulatory and
corrective influence. I'm able to judge from them how and to what
degree they appreciate what I've written.

Naturally, all writers receive mail. I'm constantly impressed by the quality of the letters I get. In those moments of self-doubt, which are legion in the life of every writer, when you wonder just who you're writing for when you sit in your hot little room stringing those beads together, if those flights of fancy are going to be too obscure for any reader, you are happily surprised to find yourself appreciated at what you thought might be your most obtuse level. Their alacrity and appreciation makes me seriously doubt that the public lacks in appetite.

N: What, to you, is the nature of humor?

Perelman: That's the roughest question of all. If you look in Fowler's *Modern English Usage* at the definitions of wit, humor, satire, and all (he has them all separated), you can become so confused you don't know which end is up.

Humor, in its simplest form, is the unexpected. Let's not go into those dreary definitions concerning a man sliding on a banana peel. Humor is the sudden disruption of thought, the conjoining of unlikely elements. It's the nostalgic reference that pleases or delights people. In my case, it is frequently a word that unlatches the past or creates a sudden picture of a past era. This is one of the reasons for choosing *Chicken Inspector #23* as the title for my most recent book. It's a reference to the sort of badge sporty young men used to wear on the lapel to flash at a girl to indicate they were pretty civilized fellows, ready for a lark. Now, I don't think anybody has mentioned those badges since I was about fifteen; they're associated with the era following the First World War. Yet I discovered in the course of writing a rather extended series for *The New Yorker* titled "Cloudland Revisited," in which I covered a lot of the books of that epoch as well as the silent films, that I was constantly amazed and gratified by the memories of readers who communicated with me after the pieces came out—the sharp images they retained of these movies and of their youths; it just needed a catalytic agent to awaken them.

N: In terms of your own sense of achievement and satisfaction, which experiences stand out as the most satisfying to you?

Perelman: One of the reasons I've worked in the theater in preference to movies or television is the fact that the theater provides the keenest distilled satisfaction a writer can get. It's immediate. I admit that the writing of a play is obviously arduous, often a bitter experience. It entails a great deal of very hard work; the writing is even more tedious and dismal. The rehearsal period is normally difficult. You rehearse in drafty, badly-lighted places, you live on cardboard cups of coffee. It's all very provisional. And what you're doing throughout this whole period of writing the play, casting it, rehearsing it, and all, can be compared to a ride on a roller coaster. You're approaching that high point on the track just before the sickening plunge. The high point is, of course, opening night. You're going up and up, and the excitement comes the morning after when you pick up those first newspapers to find out whether you've given birth to a monster or an absolutely beautiful and profitable baby. But I think the keenest satisfaction one can have is that moment of uncertainty just before you learn your fate. A first night is a very exciting thing for author and playwright. The experience of working in movies doesn't compare, because when a movie you've worked on is finally released in a whole series of theaters, you're not there to judge any effect upon the audience; it's just a lot of film.

Television seems eminently unsatisfactory. I don't see how any writer can gain any benefit out of seeing his name on the television screen, particularly since it's flanked by people rubbing floor wax into—I was about to say the ceiling; it might as well be, I guess, the floor, or becoming absolutely unglued over a deodorant, or leering over that fragrant wash. There is great satisfaction, too, in seeing a majority of your words emerge on paper, and this gets back to *The New Yorker*. I've found that the maximum of my words emerge in that one place without being butchered or manhandled or rewritten or pawed over, prayed over, or jolly well mistreated.

Now, to try to look farther, to attempt to find something in my work that is important or enduring, is frightfully difficult. I know some artists who constantly do that, and I've been exposed to their maunderings as they talk of themselves as historical figures in their own lifetimes, as Thomas Babington Macaulay. Presumptuous, isn't it?

My sole ambition is to write as well as I can in the form of the short comic essay. I've written some longer things, but I think that my shorter pieces stand the best chance of maintaining some swiftness and pace and sharpness after a few years. If a piece still stands up after four or five years, it is rather miraculous; humor does tend to date. If you look back now at the work of Artemus Ward and Josh Billings, your extremities are all a-twitch with nostalgia. Time has a corrosive effect on humor, but there is an extraordinary way in which types of humor come in and out of vogue. I get great pleasure personally from rereading the fables and slang of George Ade; he went through a curious process of becoming rather stale and démodé. But today they have a new freshness because all the slang of the early 1900s becomes fresh as you reread them.

I strayed off the point here, but what I'm trying to say is that I think it's a creditable motive for anyone who works in the vein I explore to simply hope that his work will retain some degree of freshness after a very few years. And I want to go on improving the form if I can—which amounts to a rather modest ambition.

S. J. Perelman's World
of Whimsical Wizardry

Mary Blume / 1967

From the *International Herald Tribune,* 31 May 1967. Reprinted
by permission of Mary Blume.

PARIS.—To his fans in England, America and Czechoslovakia (for
some reason he has been much translated into Czech), S. J.
Perelman is one of the best things to happen to the English language
since the Great Vowel Shift. People in other countries who don't
know his name know his work as the writer of two of the Marx
Brothers' best films, *Monkey Business* and *Horse Feathers.*

"It's a not inconsiderable achievement to have worked on two of
their pictures," said Mr. Perelman, "because people used to
swear after one that they'd rather be horsewhipped naked down the
Rue de Rivoli than do another."

The chief problems with the Marx Brothers, Mr. Perelman says,
were capriciousness and disorganization. "And Chico during
Monkey Business made several well-documented attempts to have
me fired.

"Groucho felt I was overliterary. I felt he had a wonderful talent
for parody and literary turns of speech.

"For example, in *Monkey Business* we had a love scene in a
conservatory, with Groucho reclining like Mme. Recamier. I
wanted him to leap to his feet and say, 'Come *kapellmeister,* let the
violas throb, my regiment leaves at dawn,' and then go into a
parody of *The Merry Widow* which was playing elsewhere with
Mae Murray."

Groucho left in the "Come *kapellmeister"* line but cut *The Merry
Widow* reference as too literary.

"He claimed this would be incomprehensible to what he called
the barber from Peru—by which he meant Peru, Indiana—whom
he conceived of as a mindless cretin," Perelman said.

A man whose slight frame belies his dogged courage, Perelman
spent several years as a writer in Hollywood, which he has described

as "a piquant mixture of the Main Line, the Mermaid Tavern, and any lesser French penal colony like New Caledonia." He won an Oscar for *Around the World in 80 Days* despite a running argument with Mike Todd about the word *chasm* (Todd claimed that the *ch* was pronounced as in Charlie).

Mr. Perelman is currently working on a piece about a Bentley rally he just attended in England: "I think there's material for real distortion there," he said happily. He isn't interested in further script-writing.

"Whenever I'm in an economic bind I toy with the idea and whimper to the nearest agent about my willingness to be involved, but it's not really a satisfactory situation for a writer. Of course it's better now than in the days of the big studios when the attitude was summed up by Irving Thalberg's statement: 'The writer is a necessary evil.' I thought he said weevil but I was corrected.

"As a playwright you have more power. You can withdraw the thing in a fury in New Haven and flounce out."

Perelman's plays include *One Touch of Venus,* written with Ogden Nash, and two plays written with his wife, who is the sister of Nathanael West. His latest play, *The Beauty Part,* a satire starring Bert Lahr, was a New York newspaper strike victim. "My wounds," said Mr. Perelman, "are still encapsulating."

His first book was *Dawn Ginsbergh's Revenge* in 1929—"a curious little book," Mr. Perelman recalled, "half of it was bound in old railway plush, the other half was bound in silver with hearts stamped on it." He has written regularly for *The New Yorker* since 1934.

America's leading humorist, Mr. Perelman is widely admired in England and has just made what he fears was a tedious exegesis on humor for British television.

"People do ask you about the importance of humor and with the best intentions in the world you find yourself with one hand tucked into your coat, pontificating.

"They're always asking what you think about black humor. Terry Southern, for one, leaves me calcified with boredom. It may be black, but it isn't humor."

Mr. Perelman's favorite comic essay is E. M. Forster's "Luncheon at Pretoria." *Ulysses* is his favorite comic novel: "It is without question the greatest feat of the comic imagination I have ever read."

Born in Brooklyn, Sidney Joseph Perelman moved to Rhode Island where his father was for a time an unsuccessful poultry farmer. He graduated from Brown and was first an artist especially interested in collage, then a cartoonist and then a writer.

Perelman's arrival on the literary scene was described by his good friend Robert Benchley: "Then from the Baptist precincts of Brown University wafted a cloud no bigger than a man's hams, who was S. J. Perelman. From then on, it was just a matter of time before Perelman took over the *dementia praecox* field and drove us all to writing articles on economics.'

These days Sid Perelman lives in a stone house in Bucks County, Pa., where, as he has written, he raises turkeys which he occasionally displays on Broadway.

An animal lover (he bought a dog each time he was between jobs in Hollywood), he subscribes to *La Vie des Bêtes,* once owned a mynah bird bought from a Chinese firecracker merchant in Bangkok, and currently has a standard poodle who accompanied him on a trip to Romania in search of Dracula's castle.

"She bore it with infinite patience," Mr. Perelman said. "They all wanted to know whether we wove anything from her wool."

That Perelman of Great Price Is 65

William Zinsser / 1969

As appeared in *The New York Times Magazine* 26 January 1969.

I became a teen-age addict in the late nineteen-thirties when I began
to notice in *The New Yorker* certain sentences that were unlike
any that I had ever seen before, or even imagined. They kept
turning up in pieces by a man who signed himself S. J. Perelman,
and they just plain fractured me. I memorized whole patches of
them and even started to talk in imitation of Perelmanese, a habit
that was considered attractive by nobody.

Now suddenly it is 30 years later and S. (for Sidney) J. (for
Joseph) Perelman (for Perelman) will be 65 next Saturday. He is
still doing business at the old stand; and I am still a teen-age
addict—it is only by pure will power that I can resist describing
the old stand that he is still doing business at. I'm stuck with my
adolescent crush on a writer who put the language through some
of its most breathtaking loops and, in the process, changed the
shape of 20th-century humor. Today in both America and England
the woods are full of writers and comics who were drawn into the
gravitational pull of Perelman's style and never quite got back out.

Typical of the sentences that hooked me were the following, and
anyone who doesn't think they are funny might as well get out of
the car right here and walk to the nearest article on foreign policy
or welfare. No amount of time or money will buy their good will.

> Women loved this impetual Irish adventurer who would rather fight
> than eat and vice versa. One night he was chafing at The Bit, a tavern
> in Portsmouth, when he overheard a chance remark from a brawny
> gunner's mate in his cups. . . .
>
> The following morning the "Maid of Hull," a frigate of the line
> mounting 36 guns, out of Bath and into bed in a twinkling, dropped
> downstream on the tide, bound for Bombay, object matrimony. On her
> as passenger went my grandfather. Fifty-three days later he was
> heading for the interior of one of the northern states. Living almost

45

entirely on cameo brooches and the few ptarmigan which fell to the ptrigger of his pfowling piece, he at last sighted the towers of Ishpeming, the Holy City of the Surds and Cosines, fanatic Mohammedan warrior sects.

"Jelly sandwiches! Oh, Moms!"

"Eat them all, boy o' mine," she told me, "they're good for boys with hollow little legs." Tenderly she pinned to my lapel the green tag reading "To Plushnick Productions, Hollywood, California." The whistle shrilled and in a moment I was chugging out of Grand Central's dreaming spires. I had chugged only a few feet when I realized I had left without the train, so I had to run back and wait for it to start. . . .

I noted with pleasure that a fresh coat of grime had been given to the Dearborn Street station, though I was hardly vain enough to believe that it had anything to do with my visit. . . . "General Crook," in whom I was to make my home for the next three days, and his two neighbors, "Lake Tahoe" and "Chief Malomai," were everything that the word "Pullman" implies; they were Pullmans.

The scene could have been staged only by a Lubitsch; in fact, Lubitsch himself was seated on a bench across the street, smoking a cucumber and looking as cool as a cigar. It lacked only Nelson Eddy to appear on a penthouse terrace and loose a chorus of deep-throated song, and, as if by magic, Nelson Eddy suddenly appeared on a penthouse terrace and, with the artistry that has made his name a word, launched into an aria.

"I'm sorry," he added Quigley.

"Why did you add Quigley?" I begged him. He apologized and subtracted Quigley, then divided Hogan. . . .

"Are you mad, Russell?" I stopped him haughtily. He bit his lip in a manner which awakened my maternal sympathy, and I helped him bite it.

What hooked me about these sentences was that they revealed whole new possibilities of written humor, and therefore of pleasure for the reader. I saw that anything was possible if a writer threw off the chains of logic and let his mind work by free association, ricocheting from the normal to the absurd and usually destroying, by the very unexpectedness of its angle, whatever trite or pompous idea had been there before.

I began to see that the essence of humor was surprise. Perelman would catch the reader off balance with a jagged turn and never look back. If the reader also made the turn he was a happy man, and that's what the game was all about. If he didn't there was no point in going back to pick him up; he would only miss it again.

Thus it dawned on me—and this is what has held my admiration for Perelman ever since—that a great humorist operates on a deeper current than most people suspect: pure courage. No other kind of writer risks his neck so visibly or so often on the high wire of public approval. It is the thinnest wire in all literature, and the writer lives with the certain knowledge that he will frequently fall off. Yet he is deadly serious, this acrobat teetering over our heads, or he wouldn't keep going back out, trying to startle us with nonsense into seeing our lives with sense.

For this perpetual act of courage and commitment the humorist's reward in America is to be dismissed as a trifler, someone who never settled down to "important" work. One can scan forever the list of writers who won the Pulitzer Prize or some other literary honor without finding George Ade, Ring Lardner, Robert Benchley, James Thurber, S. J. Perelman, or any other humorist.

Yet who is to say that they are not among our most valuable resources? Not me. And not, ironically, the English. Perelman is a literary hero in Great Britain. T. S. Eliot and Somerset Maugham were among his many friends and admirers there, and Spike Milligan and Peter Sellers, architects of the B.B.C.'s *Goon Show* that kept England doubled up in the fifties, acknowledge Perelman as their mentor.

In America, however, the humorist sits holding his hat at the reception desk, a queer bird, not quite to be trusted, or, above all, paid homage. Well, let other pilgrims go to Oxford, Miss., or Asheville, N.C. My own literary shrine is outside Erwinna, Pa.—and it is not hard to be outside Erwinna, Pa.—where Perelman lives in an old farmhouse with his wife, Laura, who has been his collaborator on many plays and screenplays, and two enormous poodles.

Their two grown children now live elsewhere, and the myna bird they got in Siam in 1949 has died. A spectacular attempt to redress its loss took place last year when Perelman, an avid subscriber to *La Vie des Bêtes,* noticed that his barn was exactly the length of a gibbon's swing, 34 feet, and set out to buy a pair of siamang gibbons. "I also wanted to find if there was a decent young black panther available in Bangkok," he says, "and then pick up a cheetah in East Africa on the way home." But the plan miscarried, and Perelman remains birdless and apeless in Erwinna.

There, last week, he looked back over the first 65 years of a life that has included writing movies for the Marx Brothers and sailing to Zanzibar on an Arab dhow, two adventures that he recalls with equal loathing, though, given a choice he would rather talk about the dhow. He has visited most of the exotic corners of the world that first caught his fancy in the tinted prose of Sax Rohmer and H. Rider Haggard, and perhaps no other writer—as his writings testify—has so broad and recondite a knowledge of travel. I once took a copra boat through the Moluccas solely because he told me it was a great trip (it was), and he has also steered me to interesting people in cities from Nairobi to Jakarta, sending letters ahead to ease my journey.

He is a generous man in his affection for friends and his enthusiasm for far places. "It would give me more satisfaction," he says, "to walk down Ice House Street in Hong Kong in a white drill suit than to own the Chevrolet dealership in Sheboygan, Wisc."

Reluctantly I dragged his thoughts back to Providence, where he grew up, as his fans well know from such opening sentences as this: "I'm no bloody hero, and when the Princess Pats stood at Passchendaele in '17, I was damned careful to be 12 years old and 3,000 miles to the rear, selling Domes of Silence after school to the housewives of Crescent Park, R.I."

"My father had a speckled career," he said. "He had a drygoods store and was a machinist and an unsuccessful poultryman. It was the American dream that if you had a few acres and a chicken farm there was no limit to your possible wealth. I grew up with and have since retained the keenest hatred of chickens. My chief interest always was to be a cartoonist, and I began very early to draw cartoons in my father's store on the long cardboard strips around which the bolts of Amoskeag cotton and ginghams were stored.

"I also became a great reader as soon as I was able to appreciate the beauty of Horatio Alger and Oliver Optic and books like *Toby Tyler: Or Ten Weeks with a Circus*. And there was an absolute smasher of a romantic novel called *In the Sargaso Sea*, by Janvier. I checked recently at the Providence Public Library and found that it has only been taken out twice since. I was able to recognize the very smear of chicken fat that my greasy fingers had imprisoned on the flyleaf."

At about age 11 he graduated to the material that he regards as "without question, my formative education"—the chestnuts which, long afterward, in the series called *Cloudland Revisited,* he gulped down once again and found to be chestnuts. They were books like *Graustark, Girl of the Limberlost, Trail of the Lonesome Pine, The Woman Thou Gavest, The Mystery of Dr. Fu Manchu, Three Weeks, The Winning of Barbara Worth, Scaramouche, Polly-anna,* and dozens of others beyond remembering, except by Perelman who suffers from total recall.

"It was nothing at all for people who liked reading" he says, to go to the public library on Friday with a bookstrap and bring home seven or eight books. Then you'd sit all weekend with your feet in the oven and your eyes protruding a half-inch from their sockets, wolfing ginger snaps, and finish them all. So instead of engaging in healthy blood sports, as I might have if I'd been an English boy, I was filling my mind with all this mulch."

A second layer of mulch, equally important to future growth, soon followed the first—silent films, an era symbolized in Perel-man's studio today by a photograph of Jetta Goudal. "She was the great crypto-Eurasian vampire of all time," he says. "Actually she was a Jewish girl named Yetta who took her last name from the Dutch cheese. She really ignited me in 'Java Head,' playing this tootsie who's brought back from the East Indies. I was also succes-sively in love with Corinne Griffith ('the orchidaceous star'), Priscilla Dean, Aileen Pringle and Nita Naldi, down whom, as I once wrote it was my boyhood ambition to coast on a Flexible flyer."

In 1921 Perelman went to Brown University where he found his direction by working on its humor magazine, *The Brown Jug,* as a cartoonist and later as editor. He recalls John Held Jr., as the biggest influence on college humor. "He had a deep knowledge of the flapper and the collegian and the sharpie, and he represented them in a sociological way that had tremendous humor—the flappers, for instance, in their Bramley dresses with yoke collars and accor-dion-pleated skirts and their open galoshes and their hair done in 'cootie garages' and spit curls. Held brought into focus everything that was going on with young people."

Not until mid-college did the eventual writer meet his first literary influence or try any writing. "H. L. Mencken was the Catherine wheel, the ultimate firework," Perelman says. "He loosened up journalism. With his use of the colloquial and the dynamic, the foreign reference, and the bizarre word like *Sitzfleisch* he brought adrenalin into the gray and pulpy style of the day. Under his influence I wrote editorials advocating, of course, the dismissal of the dean and all the other pompous old fools on the faculty."

Still, Perelman remained a cartoonist at heart and was thrilled, upon graduating, to get a letter from Norman Anthony, editor of *Judge*. "I tied a red bandanna to a peeled willow stick and emigrated to New York in 1925 to earn, as I believed, a sumptuous living at that magazine. I saw myself ensconced in a studio with lightly draped models, wearing a Windsor tie and a beret and expertly negotiating a palette, a loaded brush and a maulstick.

"What I didn't know was that I was hitching my star to a wagon that was gathering night soil. *Judge* was the most insolvent of magazines. Its treasurer, Joseph Cooney, had a gray suit, and they painted the office gray to make him invisible. Hirelings waiting to be paid would see a red spot moving along the wall, but by the time they realized it was Cooney's ruddy face he was out the door. I was there from 1925 to 1929 and had a contract to provide two cartoons and one humor piece every week."

Seen today, the cartoons—relying on wheezy two-liners and terrible puns—seem so callow that one wonders about the state of magazine humor in the sainted twenties. Typical is a drawing of a pasha saying to his vizier, "Who's been eating my Kurds and why?" As for the humor pieces, they aren't much better and it is not until 1930, when he went to *College Humor,* that the genuine original S. J. Perelman begins to materialize in print.

"I was beginning to develop a sense of parody and of lapidary prose," he says.

Enter the Marx Brothers. "They were feverish to get into radio," Perelman recalls, "and they detailed me and Will B. Johnstone, another comic artist, to contrive a program. We had a conception of them as four stowaways immersed in the hold of a trans-Atlantic liner, and there our invention stopped. They said, 'This

isn't our radio show, it's our next movie.' They took us up to
Jesse Lasky in the Paramount Building, and three weeks later we
were barreling westward on the Chief to write *Monkey Business.*

"Meanwhile the Marxes took off to play the Palladium in London,
where they were a dazzling failure. I can't tell you how badly
they were received—audiences threw pennies at them—which is
ironic because they're idols there today. Well, when they got back
they summoned us for a reading of our script. They came with their
lawyers and accountants and masseurs and dentists—23 people,
plus Zeppo's two Afghans and Chico's schnauzer—and I read for
85 minutes in absolute silence. At the end Chico said, 'Whaddya
think, Grouch?' Groucho took the cigar out of his mouth and said
'Stinks!' and they all got up and walked out. So we started again,
and in 1931 the picture was done and was a hit.''

The next year the Marxes signed him—and Bert Kalmar and
Harry Ruby—to write *Horse Feathers,* a comedy distinguished,
as all good Marxists know, by such exchanges as this:

SECRETARY: Jennings is waxing wroth outside.

GROUCHO: Well, tell Roth to wax Jennings for a while.

"But nothing would impel me ever to work for them again,"
Perelman says.

So began a decade of going out to Hollywood, which he once
described as "a dreary industrial town controlled by hoodlums of
enormous wealth," to work on perishable films with titles like
Florida Special and *Ambush* ("Laura and I were supposed to
introduce the humorous element"). At one point they were hired by
Irving Thalberg at M.G.M. "to work on a loathsome little thing
called *Greenwich Village* because we had once lived on Washington Square."

They also wrote such screenplays as *Sweethearts,* hardly the
most urbane of films, and Perelman once found himself put to
work on *How to Win Friends and Influence People,* intended as a
vehicle for Joan Crawford and Fanny Brice and, he says, "mercifully
never completed. Scholars today refer to the thirties as the golden
age of Hollywood. Purest nonsense. It was assembly-line stuff,
just people doing a job."

Such satisfactions as he has won in dramatic form have come
from several Broadway comedies written with his wife; from the hit

musical, *One Touch of Venus,* written with Ogden Nash; from his own play, *The Beauty Part,* and from the Academy Award-winning script of Michael Todd's *Around the World in 80 Days.* And he has his memories: of conferring with Todd around a pool in Palm Springs, for instance, and of Elizabeth Taylor "lying on a couch like Mme. Récamier, spooning in this parti-colored ice cream that an insolent Mexican chauffeur had brought nine miles and reading a copy of *The Bride Wore Black,* by Cornell Woolrich, upside down. Actually she only knows three words: Van Cleef & Arpels."

All of this, however, has been diversionary—and who is more diversionary than Elizabeth Taylor on a couch?—to the main thread of Perelman's work, the steady spinning out of humor pieces, or, as he puts it, "laboriously sewing on bugle beads." The targets of his humor have changed since he started writing for *The New Yorker* in 1934, but not the identifying marks of his style—the boundless wordplay ("my whipcores stood out like veins"), the rich invention of proper names like Lucas Membrane and the Yale Lox Associates, and the immense fund of words that are not only esoteric but precise.

"Sid commands a vocabulary," says E. B. White, "that is the despair (and joy) of every writing man. He is like a Roxy organ that has three decks, 50 stops, and a pride of pedals under the bench. When he wants a word it's there. He and Laura showed up at our house in Sarasota a couple of winters ago. They had been in an automobile accident—a bad one, the car a complete wreck. Laura came out of it with some bruises, Sid with a new word. The car, he learned, had been 'totalled.' I could see that the addition of this word to his already enormous store meant a lot to him. His ears are as busy as an ant's feelers. No word ever gets by him."

In the beginning Perelman was preoccupied, he says, with the absurdities of advertising—"Advertisers in the thirties were giving themselves the most colossal airs, bombinating away about the creative importance of what they were doing." He also dipped heavily into the pretentious world of trade magazines like *Oral Hygiene* and women's magazines like *Harper's Bazaar*—mere warm-ups, as it turned out, for a later satire that impaled the lady editor of *Flair* magazine (or was it Fleur magazine?), called "The Hand That Cradles the Rock."

"Then I got off on the nostalgia kick, revisiting the books and films of my boyhood. There was a kind of marsh gas that had begun to glow over those early movies, seen across the perspective of 25 or 30 years: a delicious humor in their crudities and their bravura. At that time, of course, there wasn't all this punditry on old films." Perelman's tolerance for today's turgid scholars of the cinema is not high. Still, it's possible that he started the whole vogue. If so, it is because he looked at his material with the special vision of the humorist and thereby saw it true—which is the greatness, he feels, of the humorists he himself most admires.

"George Ade was my first influence as a humorist," he says. "He had a social sense of history. His picture of Hoosier life at the turn of the century, as in the fable of *The Waist-Band That Was Taut,* is more documentary than any of those studies on how much people paid for their coal. Ade's humor was rooted in a perception of people and places. He had a cutting edge and an acerbic wit that no earlier American humorist had.

"Generally speaking, I don't believe in kindly humor. I don't think it exists. One of the most shameful utterances to stem from the human mouth is Will Rogers's 'I never met a man I didn't like.' The absolute antithesis is Oscar Wilde on the foxhunting Englishman: 'The unspeakable in full pursuit of the uneatable.' The two examples sum up, for me, the distinction. Wilde's remark contains, in the briefest span, the truth; whereas Rogers's is pure flatulence, crowd-pleasing, and fake humility."

Other early influences on Perelman were Stephen Leacock, Max Beerbohm, Lardner, Benchley, Donald Ogden Stewart and Frank Sullivan. A later hero was, and still is, Raymond Chandler—"He took the private-eye legend, which had been invented by Dashiell Hammett, and refined it and added an element that was not very obvious, and that was humor." (Perelman's affection for Chandler shines through his brilliant parody, "Farewell, My Lovely Appetizer.") E. M. Forster is another hero—"His story, 'Luncheon at Pretoria,' is one of the finest pieces of comic writing I know"—and so is Henry David Thoreau. "But the greatest was James Joyce.

I've come over the years to realize that *Ulysses* is the greatest work of the comic imagination that exists for me.

"Humor is purely a point of view, and only the pedants try to classify it. For me its chief merit is the use of the unexpected, the glancing allusion, the deflation of pomposity, and the constant repetition of one's helplessness in a majority of situations. One doesn't consciously start out wanting to be a social satirist. You find something absurd enough to make you want to push a couple of anti-personnel bombs under it. If it then seems to have another element of meaning, that's lagniappe. But the main obligation is to amuse yourself."

E. B. White, reflecting on Perelman's career, says, "I'm sure Sid's stuff influenced me in the early days. His pieces usually had a lead sentence, or lead paragraph, that was as hair-raising as the first big dip on a roller coaster: it got you in the stomach, and when it was over you were relieved to feel deceleration setting in. In the realm of satire, parody, and burlesque, he has, from the beginning, bowed to none. His erudition is as impressive as his flights of fancy. I don't like the word 'humorist,' never have. It seems to me misleading. Humor is a by-product that occurs in the serious work of some and not others. I was more influenced by Don Marquis than by Ernest Hemingway, by Perelman than by Dreiser."

White, of course, went on to practice many forms of writing, which he did superbly, and Benchley once claimed that he was influenced out of business altogether. "It was just a matter of time," he said, "before Perelman took over the dementia praecox field and drove us all to writing articles on economics."

So it might seem that Perelman at 65 is the last of the breed. Actually he is and always has been the only member of his breed, *sui generis* to a fault. He doesn't even look like anyone else: the copious eyebrows and mustache, the ample forehead, the thin and lively face; the small metal-rimmed glasses which he bought in Paris in 1927 and which now draw the admiring stares of hippies whose own glasses aren't as cool. His clothes are chosen, in London, with the same elegant taste that goes into his choosing of words—they are quirky but exactly right, making him that rarest of literary hands, a dapper one.

Even the trade that he plies, Perelman feels, is at the edge of extinction. ''Humor that's destined for print has almost entirely disappeared because of the growth of communication. What passes for humor on TV doesn't deserve the name.'' Nevertheless, he has started on a major work destined for print, his autobiography, to be called *The Hindsight Saga*.

Sometimes I hear people say that Perelman isn't as funny as he used to be. Who is? The early Perelman was the funniest man alive, and inevitably some of the surprise is gone because he has taught us over two generations to expect the unexpected, to stay loose. Inevitably, too, his writing has deepened with travel and scholarship; its texture is richer, its surface less gaudy.

But the biggest difference is not that humor has gone out of the humorist, but that the world has taken over his work. Life today has become so outlandish that it outstrips the writer's comic imagination. It is its own comment. Against such odds the miracle is that Perelman keeps going out on the wire. I watch him with continuing wonder and gratitude, and I wouldn't trade my addiction for anybody else's.

Appalled Perelman Going Eastward Ha!

The New York Times / 1970

The United States is about to suffer a total loss of one of its least
expendable national resources—the humorist S. J. Perelman.

Mr. Perelman has made an apparently irrevocable decision to
move to London in October, there to live as a self-exiled American. He will become a "resident alien," with no expectation of
returning to the nation in which he has won acclaim as lampoonist laureate.

The 91-acre farm in Bucks County, Pennsylvania, that he and his
brother-in-law, the late Nathanael West, bought in 1932 has been sold,
and its contents will be auctioned at the site on September 25. Mr.
Perelman will live here briefly until he sails for London on October 21.

"The fact that I think it's volcano time in this country is not
responsible for the move, though I'm just as appalled as everyone
about the conditions," the 66-year-old Mr. Perelman said when
reached by telephone at the farm, near Erwinna, Pennsylvania,
where he was packing about 1,000 of his books for storage.

"I've had all of the rural splendor that I can use," he said, "and
each time I get to New York it seems more pestilential than
before. I think Swift said that life is not only nasty and brutish, but
short. That seemed to me the perfect description of life in a
termitary like New York.

"Plants can live on carbon dioxide, but I can't. I think T. S. Eliot
used the phrase 'twice breathed air.' I'd hesitate to say how many
times the air in New York has been rebreathed."

Mr. Perelman said the nation was afflicted with "insanity and
violence," symptoms of jingoism, and rampant political fatuous-
ness. Its citizens cultivate manners that are scant on couth, he said,
noting that incivility was a plague for which there was no anti-
toxin.

He confessed that he was disaffected with the American political climate "all the way down from the co-author of the Mundt-Nixon bill—I won't specify which sponsor I mean—to every hard-hat and redneck in this country."

He spent four months in London last winter and found there what seemed "a far more rational society than our own."

"The obvious good manners and consideration of people there toward each other may be only selfish, but it's good enough for me," he said.

Mr. Perelman's wife of nearly 40 years, Laura West Perelman, died on April 10. He said that she had agreed with him about three years ago to move to London.

The author of 18 books of satire (including *Parlor, Bedlam, and Bath* in 1930, *Westward Ha!* in 1948 and *The Ill-Tempered Clavichord* in 1953) and the creator of scores of improbable characters was born Sidney Joseph Perelman in Brooklyn in 1904.

He was reared in Rhode Island and educated at Brown University, where he edited *The Brown Jug*.

He started in 1925 as a comic artist for the magazine *Judge*. "The captions on my drawings got longer and longer, and soon they displaced the drawings," he said.

Two Marx Brothers pictures, *Monkey Business* and *Horse Feathers* rank high among his screenplays.

He said that after his move these would be no diminution in the United States of his writings. He will continue to write for *The New Yorker* from London and he expects that his books will appear at irregular intervals.

He added, "Today the news in this country is so filled with insanity and violence that the newspapers, from which I derive many of my ideas, have scant room for the sort of thing that turns me on—the bizarre, the unusual, the eccentric. In Britain they still have the taste for eccentricity."

Pun and Names with S. J.

Myra MacPherson / 1970

As appeared in the *Providence Sunday Journal* 25 October 1970, from The Washington Post News Service. Reprinted by permission of *The Washington Post*.

It was 1930 when S. J. Perelman ran afoul of the Marx Brothers.

A brief backstage encounter with Groucho, appearing on Broadway in *Animal Crackers,* got Perelman the job of collaborating with Will B. Johnstone on a movie script.

Perelman, then 26 and the writer of a few published humorous works, signed up for $300 a week and headed for that city he learned to loathe, Hollywood.

Perelman and Johnstone concocted a 135-page script, "Full of jargon—'medium close shots' and all that, not quite understanding it," Perelman recalled. The time came for Perelman to read the screenplay. Into the room strolled Harpo, Chico, Zeppo, Groucho, "their wives, three afghans, a schnauzer, lawyers, dentists, outriders."

"There were 23 people and this thing was a blood bath," Perelman recalled. "I read to complete silence. Finally, I lost my voice altogether and whispered whole portions."

One and one-half hours later he ended, to deafening silence.

"Then," Perelman recalls, "Chico turned to Groucho and said, 'What do you think?' Groucho plucked the cigar from his lips and said, 'Stinks.' "

With that, Groucho rose and was immediately followed by all the others in the room, still silent. Perelman went home.

"The only thing that prevented me from throwing myself out the window was the fact I was in a first-floor bungalow," he remembers.

The Marx Brothers were eventually subdued and after five months more work on the script, out came *Monkey Business.* Perelman stayed around to write *Horse Feathers.* Through the years, during intermittent lapses from writing pieces for *New Yorker* and other

magazines, Perelman returned to Hollywood screen plays, among
them, *Around the World in 80 Days*.

Today, at 66, Perelman is a dapper man with a neatly clipped
mustache, silver-rimmed glasses, unrumpled clothes that match
(brown and blue houndstooth checked jacket, blue shirt, brown
shoes) and total recall of the ups and downs in his own career
viewed with a humorous detachment.

He is back in the news again for two reasons. One is the publication of his latest collected humor, *Baby, It's Cold Inside*. The
other is that Perelman, for years a disguised Anglophile, recently
became an undisguised one. He is going to live in England where
he feels the climate is right for him to create his pun-filled humor.

"There they still have a taste for eccentricity," he explained.

Some of Perelman's statements regarding his departure can sound
disturbingly crotchety, perhaps with a tinge of sour grapes disenchantment of a man whose humor style is foreign to the buying
young. The book jacket spiel aims at an older market—"You don't
need to strip naked to enjoy it. Or sit on the floor. Or wear
love beads."

"As a glittering generality, reality has overtaken fantasy. One
great problem for comic writers is that life today surpasses any
fantasy you can think of. Almost everything is so bizarre." This
goes for the more serious afflictions he sees here—violence,
symptoms of jingoism and rampant incivility to the fashion of
the times.

"Clothes have disappeared. Everyone is in costume. When you
see your exterminator riding in on the train with you, carrying his
English attache case, wearing a hat that looks like a cone of ice
cream, and those great flowing sideburns what fantasy could one
write that's any funnier?"

Another problem for writers, Perelman feels is what he terms "the
great phenomena of our age—the decline of reticence. Everyone has
got to express everything. There are no secrets any more. This is
particularly true of sexual relations. We've reached the point where
it's like supermarket goods. I believe in reticence in all things."

He understandably had difficulty being amused by such true-
confessions humor as Philip Roth's *Portnoy's Complaint*.

"I found that book boring," he says. "After 40 pages I just could

not go on. The function of a writer is to convey the furtherest
degree of sexuality without being specific. He fails in his duty as a
writer when he has to resort to four and five-letter words. The
belief of young writers that they can induce shock by four-letter
words that have become as common as "milk" and "salt" is fatuous.

"What is interesting to speculate about—and I often discuss this
with people like William Shawn (*New Yorker* editor) is: Just as
when the freedom of the restoration was followed by the repression
of puritanism—whether we're going to go back to puritanism."

"The American political climate—all the way down from the co-
author of the Mundt-Nixon bill—I won't specify which sponsor I
mean—to every hard-hat and redneck in this country," disturbs
him. So does Vice President Agnew (who gets help with his
speeches from other humorists—Bob Hope's gag writers). "The
dangerous thing is Agnew is articulate and cold. He doesn't get
excited and handles himself ably and skillfully."

While Perelman was at it, he brought up another bothersome
point, the "dehumanization in our society. The other day I noticed an
advertising man said 'I'm programmed' to meet this person."

"I'd be grateful if you stress the fact that I had contemplated this
move three years ago. It's really an unemotional plan," he says.
"I hate the word expatriate; I plan to remain a non-resident of the
United States and return as frequently as possible. I'll get the air
mailed newspaper from here."

Perelman was asked how he felt England—with its own share of
the mod, the way-out, the youthquake, the hippie scene—would
be a refuge for a man who is a "great admirer of clean hair
and couth."

Perelman answered: "In England that scene is confined to a
certain segment of the population. The older person is respected
always much more there. The English still cleave more to values
and traditions of the past. In America the youth cult is pushed
more and more to the forefront."

Another reason is that he feels the English are "mad for" the
puns he loves, long considered the lowest form of humor in
American creative writing courses. (Who could forget that title
Nobody Knows the Rubble I've Seen? "Nobody knows but Croesus.")

Perelman's wife of 40 years, Laura West, sister of the late

Nathanael West, died last April. This spurred him into selling
their farm in Bucks County, Pennsylvania, purchased by Perelman
and West in 1932.

An auction at the farm a few weeks ago was attended by 500
strangers and neighbors. Mr. X, a brown horse, was bought for
$80, by a woman who said she's paid $40 too much for it. Two
movie manuscripts went for $7 and an English-made, four-door
black 1963 Rover brought $1,300.

Perelman said he had no regrets about leaving the farm. "I went
through a big Thoreau phase when every drop of water on every
fern seemed to be terribly significant. It wore off a good many
years ago."

West was a class ahead of Perelman at Brown University, and
when Perelman met West's sister, "I found her very pleasing and
eventually married her. The three of us were a very tight-knit
organism." West's work was often bitterly scathing but Perelman
said that in person, "He was extremely outgoing and gregarious—as
well as visionary. *A Cool Million* seems very relevant now, what
with the stirrings of what we can only hope is not fascism."

Perelman was born Sidney Joseph. "I hated my first name and
simply retired it to anonymity. My father was an immigrant in
1892, with dreams of becoming an engineer."

His father never got his chance to go to college and "become
third engineer on a steamer—the first ship into Havana Harbor
after the sinking of the Maine. His was an interesting and difficult
life; he worked in factories and a dry goods store in Providence."

Perelman started his career as a comic artist—but then the
captions got so long they began to overtake the drawings. "I began
drawings when I was very small—first on those rectangle cardboard
things that were always inside bolts of cloth that came to the dry
goods store." Perelman's father "eventually realized the great
American dream and became a chicken farmer. We found ourselves in rural Rhode Island." He remembers this as a "terrible
poor" period. The hens "perished always in the first east wind
after their birth."

But Perelman got a good education. His love for the four-sylla-
ble—rather than the four-letter—word started when he attended
Classical High School, where he had four years of Latin and three

of Greek. "I was very fond of reading and gave myself tremendous airs. I was an early discoverer of Joyce, who I venerated." (Perelman has 11 copies of *Ulysses* and could not bear to part with any of them at the auction.)

Perelman has some unflattering things to say about much of the youth movement in movies and particularly the amount of space turned over to "the gods and goddesses," the movie reviewer, even in the *New Yorker*. "In the old days Ross never believed movies were a valid art. If a review ran over one paragraph he became very restive. I think page on page is extremely boring."

Perelman is amused by young filmmakers. "The 'professionalism' of young movie makers is a source of sardonic pleasure. They're all so much more technical, talk of truck shots and whip shots. Then what turns out are what we called 'chasers'—snow melting, a little Chopin tinkling behind it. They're sort of playing at it and giving themselves enormous seriousness about the whole thing."

Perelman is pleased, in the face of this to see revivals of the Marx and W. C. Fields movies.

One of the things that prompted Perelman's move from Bucks County to England rather than to New York City is the daily struggle to move in Manhattan.

"The exasperation, the trembling with hatred. To me, the prototype is to be frozen in a taxi on West 34th on a hot August day, the taxi driver in his undershirt, the stench of gasoline, you're one half hour late for an appointment, the driver's wrath at cops and trucks turns on you. It's a scene only Hogarth could portray."

Or, perhaps, an S.J. Perelman essay.

S. J. Perelman Takes a Powder

Robert Taylor / 1970

The Boston Globe, 22 November 1970. Reprinted by courtesy of *The Boston Globe.*

I'm walking out the door like Thoreau,'' said S. J. Perelman. "Unafraid and empty-handed.''

It was not quite true. Perelman had copies of Joan Didion's *Slouching Toward Bethlehem* and L. E. Sissman's *Scattered Returns* and *Dying: An Introduction,* in his room at the Ritz. He admires both Miss Didion, a California novelist and essayist, and the Boston poet. Going out, he would walk unafraid and empty-handed and well-dressed and literate, a rare combination these days, but not surprising in context.

S. J. (for Sidney Joseph) was—and one presumes, still is—the literary idol of my generation. Bookworms of that unashamedly decadent era seldom hailed writers for high-toned ethical and mystical qualities (in fact, these constituted serious drawbacks) but for linguistic powers. And in the linguistic sphere Perelman, after the death of Joyce, reigns supreme. What young blade in quest of pseudo-sophistication—the only kind worth having—did not hoard his share of apt Perelmanisms winnowed either from the collected works or from the immortal movies S. J. wrote for the Marx Brothers— *Monkey Business* and *Horse Feathers?* "Here is my card and a report of my recent urinalysis.'' "Gentlemen. I give you Martha Custis, hetman of the Don Cossacks, her feature social with the fragile beauty of a cameo.'' "From the steaming jungles of the Gran   to the snows of Kanchan   from the Hook of Holland is the Great Barrier Reef, the white dot on the Buntwell pipe stem is the sign of the sahib.''

If the man who wrote those words was taking a powder, clearly the country was in deeper trouble than any mumbling Cassandra of the current scene has predicted. Perelman had just sold his 91-acre farm in Bucks County, Pa. The farm, where the Perelmans have lived for years, was purchased from Michael Gold. Hardly a New

Masses subscriber now alive still reads Mike Gold, author of moving
and sensitive screeds *(Jews Without Money)* as well as reams of the
dreariest propaganda. Proletarian laureates like Gold always seemed
to end up in Bucks County, or working for M-G-M, or in the
Kremlin Wall. Which indicates how far the Perelman roots ex-
tend, intertwined with the roots of the Republic.

The reports of S. J.'s exodus though, also turned out to be
exaggerated. "I'm not settling in England as an expatriate," he
explained. "The *Times* heard about the auction of effects after we
sold the farm, and the reporter who called up must have been wearing
a leaky headset. He got me standing in the rubble, at an uncomfortable moment, anyway, I intend to come back here frequently and
continue this shabby little trade of mine."

"You are quoted as saying that it's 'volcano time' in the US," he
was told.

"The fact that I think it's volcano time is not responsible for the
move. I'm just as appalled as anyone else at insanity and violence.
London's a more rational setting." Perelman groped in the pockets
of his sports jacket and produced a crumpled Lucky. "I've
reached a point where I regard my existence as an artichoke and
I'm stripping away the outer layers."

"A certain disenchantment with the political climate may be
considered part of it?"

Perelman nodded. "When I was a kid my parents used to drag
me around to draughty halls in Providence to listen to people like
A. J. Muste. I'm afraid there isn't the same kind of sympathy for
nonconformists today."

"But yahoos and rednecks aren't the only reason?"

"Do you really want to know why I'm moving to England?" He
lit the Lucky, but paused, and the match nearly scorched his
fingers. "They don't finish sentences in England. They telegraph
the thought. People speak in ellipses. They don't need to finish
sentences because they're on the same wavelength."

"Well, you're saying good-bye to a lot of passionate intensity."

"Clive Barnes warned me not to idealize the English, but there
was a homesick note when he said it. The eccentric, the individual
and the bizarre still have a place. The last time I was in London I

dropped into Alexander Smith's on Oxford Street. Smith's, as
you probably know, sells walking sticks. I asked the clerk for a
Penang Lawyer. Of course, a Penang Lawyer is the cane em-
ployed by Sherlock Holmes at Stoke Moran, the house of Dr.
Grimesby Roylott, during the *Adventure of the Speckled Band.*
The clerk looked at me and without changing expression, said:
'You, sir, are the eleventh American who's inquired after a Penang
Lawyer this year.' If that isn't reason enough to move to Knights-
bridge, what is?''

> "I was making a decent living writing fugitive pieces for the magazines,
> pieces which while not pretentious, I and others of my ilk fondly
> imagined could be turned into thirty dollars here or forty dollars there. It
> was a perfectly good racket, at any rate.
>
> "Then, from the Baptist precincts of Brown University, wafted a cloud
> no bigger than a man's hams, who was S. J. Perelman. From then on,
> it was just a matter of time before Perelman took over the dementia
> praecox field and drove us all to writing articles on economics for *The
> Commentator.*"
>
> —Robert Benchley

"As you probably know," "as you doubtless know," "as you
know already"—these are operative phrases in Perelman's lexi-
con. Possessing what is unquestionably the widest range of allusion
of any writer extant, he takes pains to indicate that his conversation
is courteously crossindexed. When he mentions Sherlock Holmes,
the New York literary scene of the twenties and thirties, old
movies, any of his 18 books, from *Dawn Ginsbergh's Revenge,* of
1929, to the latest *Baby, It's Cold Inside,* which appeared to
front-page hosannas in *The Sunday Times Book* section a few weeks
ago, Perelman manipulates the allusion to suggest intimacy rather
than the flaunting of specialized knowledge. For instance, he is
fascinated by the dandyism of bespoke clothing, and refers to
Nihleen, the custom bootmaker, leaving oxblood-hued shoes in a
sunny window in order to secure a green-olive patina (S. J.'s own
bootmaker, for the record, is George Cleverly of Cork Street, and
his tailor is Anderson and Sheppard). His interest in such recondite lore is never snobbish; the accent of Brooklyn still tinges
Perelman's diphthongs; and indeed his interest may be professional, since the use of shop talk and jargon forms part of his material.

"I once had an agent named Mark Hanna," he says, adding that was Mark's true name and the agent was what used to be known as "a snappy dresser." "One day I came into his office and he said, 'Stop right there.' I was wearing a new coat made by a tailor he'd recommended. 'Turn sideways,' he said. 'Hmm, not bad.' Then he walked around his desk and examined the inside of the coat. 'Sid,' he said, 'show me a man who can bushel a seam like that these days.' "

Bushel a seam . . . the pure Perelmania. S. J. is presently writing his autobiography, which he intends to call *The Hindsight Saga.* The title has been pirated in one version or another ever since the maestro announced it during an interview; Perelman doesn't care—he feels that his announcement gave him prior claim, even though there's no way to copyright a title. Originally he wanted to call it *Smiling, the Boy Fell Dead,* but his wife Laura objected on grounds of morbidity.

Born in Brooklyn, Perelman grew up in Providence. His presence is still very much felt in Brown University tradition, for he was a member of the class of '25, a class associated with Perelman, his brother-in-law Nathanael West, who wrote *Miss Lonelyhearts* and *The Day of the Locust,* and writer Israel James Kapstein, author of the novel *Something of a Hero,* and later a distinguished English professor at Brown.

While he was going to college, Perelman managed a cigar store on Washington Street, just above Fay's Theater, the hustings where he first caught the Marx Brothers. "They had a rancid little vaudeville act with Leo (Perelman tends to think of the Marxes as Leo and Julius rather than Chico and Groucho and company) shooting the piano, and that sort of thing, and I thought they were very funny."

At this stage of his career, however, Perelman regarded himself as a cartoonist rather than a writer. His models were John Held and Ralph Barton. It was an era of remarkable talent appearing in undergraduate humor magazines. One evening at the cigar counter Perelman eavesdropped on the conversation of a couple of cake-eaters whom he deduced were strays from Columbia. "If you're from Columbia," he put in, "do you know Corey Ford?" (Ford's

work then enlivened *The Columbia Jester*.) "I am Corey Ford,"
one of the customers answered. This impressed Perelman more than
meeting the Marx Brothers and does to this day. The store shut
down and the Prohibition scotch came open.

As cartoonist S. J. Perelman went to New York, and, between 1925
and 1929, contributed pen-and-wash drawings to *Judge*. "I had
four distinct manners," he says. "Held, Barton, figures based on
African sculpture, then I hit upon collage which no one else was doing
in cartoons then. From African sculpture I had learned the efficacy
of repetition. I introduced repetitive elements: if a big business-
man was drawn, I'd clip out the stock market quotations for his
vest. Next, I began using dress materials. I'd go down to the
garment district and ask for swatches; they probably thought I was
as queer as Dick's hatband, but all the same it was an early
American use of collage technique."

Perelman never illustrated any of his own later books, which
often had jackets by E. McKnight Kauffer, a well-known English
poster artist. Nevertheless, it was the visual arts that gave rise to
Dawn Ginsbergh's Revenge. Perelman had become immersed in
old advertising illustrations, and more or less wrote the text to
complement the pictures, thus establishing at one stroke, an
inimitable style. "As publication day loomed, I grew more and
more excited. Finally, the books arrived from Horace Liveright.
The binding was flock, a kind of green railroad-plus color, and with
trembling hands I opened to the title page. Dawn Ginsbergh's
Revenge, Horace Liveright and Company—no clue whatsoever as
to the name of the author. If it wasn't stamped on the book's
spine, you'd never know."

Dawn Ginsbergh (today the scarcest of Perelman items, with a
retail price of $50 on the rare book market) marks the terminus of
Perelman's cartooning ambitions. He left *Judge* and worked for
College Humor, but as a writer. And during that year occurred
the momentous collision with the Marxes.

"My father-in-law had given my wife and me tickets to their
Broadway production of *Animal Crackers*. At the interval I sent
back a card to Groucho. He'd read some of my stuff, it turned out,

and he sent back an invitation to meet him in his dressing-room after the show.

"We went back, and in short order Groucho got down to business. Radio was big then, all kinds of show business types were getting rich, and the Marx Brothers didn't want to miss the gold rush. Groucho asked me if I'd collaborate with Will Johnstone and write some radio scripts. At the end of six days all that Will and I had was the notion of the four Marxes as stowaways in barrels on a transatlantic liner. Groucho sent for us. When we arrived he introduced Jesse Lasky who told us we weren't writing the next Marx Brothers broadcast; we were writing the next Marx Brothers movie. Overnight the scene shifted to the West Coast. Neither Will nor I had any notion of what a film scenario was supposed to look like, and the script of *Monkey Business,* was crammed with the most elaborate technical directions, 'iris down,' 'lip dissolve,' 'dolly over'."

Perelman's memories of the Marxes are anything but nostalgic. They drive him to expletive, and he is not a man to deploy expletive. "In Hollywood I was a novelty, pointed out to rubber-necking tourists as the man who managed to endure two consecutive films with the Marx Brothers. *The Hindsight Saga* deals with the boys in a chapter called 'The Winsome Foursome.' One of the traumas of my life was reading aloud the scenario of *Horse Feathers* to the Brothers, their accountants, their barber, their dentists, as-sorted relatives and members of the entourage, 27 persons in all and five dogs, each of whom heard the gags in glum silence.

"I always viewed Hollywood from the standpoint of a freebooter, however. If I got three thousand dollars for script we'd go to Paris and blow the wad. My object all sublime was to beat the Holly-wood idea."

Although he was to work in Hollywood intermittently for three decades (Perelman received the Academy Award in 1957 for his script of *Around the World in 80 Days),* the process of detachment was underway. The Perelmans were now collaborating on plays, S. J. contributing sketches to such entertainments as *Walk A Little Faster,* with Bobby Clark and Beatrice Lillie. And the humorous idylls, an output without parallel for variety and savor, had begun gracing the *New Yorker.*

> Yes, despite his appearance, he was really a very complicated young
> man with a whole set of personalities, one inside the other like a nest
> of Chinese boxes. And "The Burning of Los Angeles," a picture he was
> soon to paint, definitely proved he had talent.
>
> —Nathanael West

Perelman, en route to autograph books at the Harvard Coop,
Storrow Drive ramps flowing past, discusses his brother-in-law
Nathanael West and his wife, Eileen—the subject of the book *My
Sister Eileen,*—who were killed in a California automobile crash
in December, 1940, the day after F. Scott Fitzgerald had dropped
dead. Perelman thinks it probable that West, who had been on
vacation, hunting in Mexico, had heard the news about Fitzgerald,
and was rushing home. "I met West at Brown after he transferred
from Tufts in '23. He advanced daring notions. One of them was
that we ought to disguise ourselves with ticking aprons and walk
into the John Hay library, where there was an elephant folio of
Hogarth. We'd carry table legs. West's idea was to nail the folio
onto the table legs, and if anyone stopped us, we'd say we were
moving a coffee table. I pointed out to him the nails would spoil
the volume, so we dropped the scheme. Who wants a Hogarth folio
with nail holes?"

"Why did the pair of you want the Hogarth in the first place?"
he was asked.

"Decadent aestheticism," Perelman says, with a wry smile. He
is West's literary executor, and each year eager doctoral candi-
dates seek exclusive rights to the unpublished materials.

The talk roams lightly to other subjects, to movie tycoons like
Harry Cohn, who thought Perelman was an erudite chocolate
candy manufacturer named Sam from San Francisco (" 'Sam,' he
said one day, 'what kind of a movie would Irwin Shaw's *The
Young Lions* make?' Naturally, he hadn't read the book; they never
did. 'You'll make millions, Harry,' I said.") To Billy Wilder, the
director, who has spent the last three-and-a-half years doing *The
Private Life of Sherlock Holmes,* a picture which Perelman,
deeply versed as he is in Holmes, feels is a potential masterpiece
("It concentrates on the relationship between the two men. For
instance, Watson is worried, as a doctor, about Holmes's cocaine
dosage, and tries to find out where Holmes has hidden his

supply.'') To the Algonquin Round Table (''I came along at the end
of that. It was what the French called 'cuisoniere,' cooked. You'd
think of a wisecrack days in advance then try to steer the conversation around for an opening.'') To A. J. Liebling, another *New
Yorker* contributor (''Liebling once said of Joe Mitchell. 'He's a
very careful writer'—the greatest form of praise I think any writer
ever received from another.'') But as the car turns into the Larz
Anderson Bridge. Perelman is again talking of West.

"He was the night manager for the Hotel Sutton off Times
Square, and he'd get his literary buddies over there. Dashiell
Hammett wrote *The Thin Man* at the Sutton. Dash had run up a
tremendous bar bill at the Pierre, where he was living, so West
invited him to come and stay. As you undoubtedly know, Dash was
almost the prototype of the Thin Man, a tall, angular fellow. He
got out of the Pierre wearing some six suits and four overcoats, the
manager didn't give him a second glance. At the Sutton he stuck
to a rigid schedule devised by West. One beer a day and one page a
day. At the end of 365 days he'd finished his book."

Crossing Harvard Square, Perelman is bemused by the swirl of
exotic fauna, crowds drifting around and looking for all the world
like dress extras in a production of *The Day of the Locust*. Inside
the Coop, stacks of *Baby, It's Cold Inside* rise next to stacks of a
book called *The 100 Most Important People in the World Today*.
Perelman ignores this; as he signs, he is asked about humor today.

"My line of descent, as I see it, is Stephen Leacock, George Ade,
Ring Lardner, Benchley, Donald Ogden Stewart and Frank Sullivan. Good humor really doesn't spoil; I can still read Ade with
pleasure, although most of the references are dated. As for my
work. I recommend reading a little of it at a time. They're not books
you're supposed to devour from cover to cover. You take them in
small doses, the way you'd take a liqueur."

Perelman finished autographing *Baby, It's Cold Inside*. At the
entrance of the Coop he paused and carefully scrutinized a window
display of Andrew Wyeth reproductions. "I hope you admire this
man as much as I do." Then Perelman joined the welter of the
square. In context, saris, granny dresses, dungarees, buckskins and
sans culotte operetta costumes, he looked flamboyant, an individual in the crowd—*he's a very careful writer*—walking out.

Lumpen Doyen of Hollywood Wits

John Hall / 1970

As appeared in *The Manchester Guardian*, 30 November 1970:8.

I have often toyed with the notion of retailing for public consumption a historic little fable which I once received, first-hand, from the son of a Harrar skin trader. This aged gentleman, who lost one arm to the crocodiles, and was therefore obliged to pass on all of his historic fables first-hand, told me of a meeting which he once had with the expatriate Rimbaud, whom he knew to be a dilettante poetaster gone sour. Asked for an account of his dealings with a kinsman, name of Verlaine, the exscribe apparently racked his brain cruelly and finding it was not what it used to be, murmured, "Verlaine? Verlaine? Don't tell me. Wasn't he from Encyclopedia Brittanica? No, I tell a lie; he was the one from Aspreys, tried to sell me a Colt repeater. Either way, his salesmanship was merde."

The occasion for the release of this poignant vignette, which I have hitherto concealed like the black tulip, a ticket for Night of Nights, or more accurately, like a transparent lie, is that I just heard a stunningly parallel tale of the crossed wires of high art, a first-lip yarn from the distrait protagonist in one of this century's greatest, most tempestuous literary link-ups. Which is to say, I'm fresh from the feet of S. J. Perelman (literally, since he obviously rolled off the ottoman in his nightdress when I rang the bell, and failed to encounter his slippers en route for the door).

The quiet, talkative, steel-rimmed, urbane, lumpen doyen of Hollywood and *New Yorker* witsters who greeted me was subtly different from the quiet, talkative, steel-rimmed doyen I had expected to find in that he wasn't wearing trousers. Discreetly, he ushered me to a bottle of Maxim freeze-dried American coffee and suggested I should drink as freely as I pleased while he returned to bed for half an hour. Which gave me chance to muse over the following brief list of the maestro's achievements, concealed with nonchalant professionalism in an open copy of his complete works on the adjacent hallstand.

So this was S. J. Perelman, Brooklyn born and Brown educated; author of 17 books, four plays, and many films, including the Marxes' *Monkey Business* and *Horse Feathers* (if it wasn't I was in the wrong house). Perelman of *Dawn Ginsbergh's Revenge, Strictly From Hunger, Crazy Like a Fox, Westward Ha!, The Ill-Tempered Clavichord,* and latterly, *Baby It's Cold Inside* (Weidenfeld, 35s) which was my entrée, and full flavoured at that. Perelman, who has vouchsafed to us a description of himself and his work as follows:

"I was a balding, presbyopic individual with a ragged handlebar moustache and a complexion the colour of beetroot who, lacking the adroitness to pickpockets, was forced to become a writer." He was a notably nonathletic youth who gave himself blinding headaches each weekend by overindulgence in pulp literature, which he browsed while propping his feet on the family stove and consuming biscuits to the point of acute constipation. Of his university years, he has said:

"For six months after seeing Erich von Stroheim in *Foolish Wives,* I exhibited a maddening tendency to click my heels and murmur *Bitte?* along with a twitch as though a monocle were screwed into my eye. The mannerism finally abated, but not until the Dean of Brown University had taken me aside and confided that if I wanted to transfer to Heidelberg, the faculty would not stand in my way."

And of his years as a Hollywood scriptwriter: "I gained my livelihood writing for the silver screen, an occupation which, like herding swine, makes the vocabulary pungent but contributes little to one's prose style."

As I was only the thirty-seventh journalist to interview Perelman since he came to live in London a month ago, I was naturally bursting to hear a mint account of his meeting and work with the Marx brothers, and of the Hollywood scene of the thirties. In the event, the account turned out to have something of the flavour of Rimbaud's riposte, in that it concerned a partnership well worth forgetting. After he had slopped into something loose and clinging, Mr. Perelman went to his muttons in the following wise:

"I had a tentative acquaintance with Groucho, in that he appar-

ently liked my writing for *Judge* and *College Humour* in the
twenties, and when my first book was published, he supplied an
arresting blurb, which ran like this: 'This is a marvelous book.
From the moment I picked it up to the moment I laid it down, I was
suffused with laughter. Someday I intend reading it.' Anyway,
my wife and I had a couple of ducketts to see the Marxes' Broadway
musical *Animal Crackers,* and we were so diverted by this that we
sent a card backstage at the interval, announcing the fact.

"Well, we were invited to go round and meet the artists, and my
wife was rather unhorsed by what she saw, because the Marxes
were running around in their undershorts and goosing showgirls,
and that was a scene she wasn't very well clued into. This was the era
of the great radio comedians, Eddie Cantor, Ed Wynn, Fred Allen,
Jack Benny, and so on. They were all making a great deal of
money, and the Marxes, being avaricious, wanted some of this loot,
and the substance of this visit was that they wanted me to think
out some radio programmes for them.

"They coupled me with a New York newspaper man called Will
Johnstone, and the two of us sat about trying to scratch up some
idea for a radio programme, and the only thing that occurred to us
was that the brothers might be stowaways, each in his own barrel,
on a transatlantic liner. Beyond that, our inspiration failed, and for
two or three days we just sat there. Then to our horror, the
Marxes bade us to lunch at the Hotel Arbor, where we showed up,
and rather gingerly presented our idea. And to our great surprise,
Groucho looked at Chico and said: 'This isn't our radio programme,
it's our next picture.' And they took us both by all hands and led
us down to the Paramount building."

Two weeks later, Perelman, Johnstone, their respective wives,
and three jugs of corn liquor entrained for the West Coast, Johnstone
heard that there was no alcohol to be had west of the continental
divide, and he was so frightened by the idea that he secured the
three crocks. That was the beginning of Perelman's Hollywood
adventures, which ran to two Marx Brothers films and ten years
of mainly "B" movies for Paramount. How did he find the Marxes?

"As far as temperaments and their personalities were concerned,
they were capricious, tricky beyond endurance, altogether unreli-
able, and treacherous to a degree that would make Machiavelli

absolutely kneel at their feet. They were also megalomaniac to a
degree which is impossible to describe, despite the fact that they
were not yet what they were to become after these pictures.

"I did two films with them, which in its way is perhaps my
greatest distinction in life, because anybody who ever worked on
any picture for the Marx Brothers said he would rather be chained
to a galley oar and lashed at ten minute intervals until the blood
spurted from his frame than ever work for these sons of bitches
again.

"How did I survive? Well, it was the idea that I wanted to go on
eating, really. To give you an idea of the forms of their treachery, I
remember that when Johnstone and I arrived on the West Coast,
the Marxes were being hosted at the London Palladium (it's taken
40 years for this sort of humour to get through, and they weren't
appreciated then). Chico sent a cable to Paramount, saying 'Feel
that the writers in Hollywood are untrained, naive (and a string of
various denunciations). Replace at once.' Of course, they had no
idea what we were doing. We had left with thorough approval of the
basic idea, and we were working away like beavers.

"True we were amateurs, who didn't know pictures, so we
crammed every bit of technical jargon we knew into this thing.
We had medium close shot, camera irises down on, camera trucks
to, camera workapiches around . . . It eventually became my
calvary that I had to read this thing to 27 people, of whom the
Marxes were only four, naturally, the other 23 being auditors,
relatives, assistant producers, insurance men, two Afghan hounds
and a Schnauzer. The wonder was we weren't torn to pieces by
the dogs; we certainly were by everyone else, and we thought this
was the end of our relationship. But oddly enough, we were called
back in, and this thing became the basis, after eight months' work,
of *Monkey Business*."

Perelman stayed with Paramount until 1942, working as a script-
ing team with his wife, Laura. The idea was that a husband and
wife team would go on discussing work when they got home; S. J.
and Laura imposed a 3 p.m. curfew, after which they could talk
about anything but the script. They survived the sham and glamour
of the place by working until they had raised enough for a trip to

France, where they holed up until the wrinkles reappeared in the
bellies. Then they returned and went through the process again.

"We detested Hollywood, but it was the only place we knew to
make a living. I survived because I was young, and a little of the
glamour still clung to the place. At first blush, Hollywood seems to
be paradisiacal. The grass is green; the flowers don't smell but
the women do. But then you realise it's Bridgeport with palms. It's
the city of dreadful day. My peculiar fascination with Los Angeles
was the style of the city's murders. *Double Indemnity* summed it
up. The motive, the method, and everything else about that city's
murders had the two-dimensional quality of American life."

A friend of both Chandler and Dashiell Hammett, Perelman
admired their style, and tried his own hand more than once at a
Hollywood gangster. *Ambush* was a Laura and S. J. Perelman
script.

"This was about a bank mob that works out an original way of
knocking over a bank, and we thoroughly enjoyed this because
the values were real and solid. Some hoods grab the loot and away
they go, the police after them. There are no big psychological
questions, no sturm und drang about the motivation. Just plain,
real values."

Outside Hollywood, he divided his time between magazine writing and Broadway, where his best-remembered shows were *All
Good Americans, The Night Before Christmas,* and *One Touch of
Venus* (in collaboration with Ogden Nash for Kurt Weill's music).
But the outlet for his finest flights of bizarre, cultured wit were
magazines like *Holiday, New Yorker, Venture,* and *TV Guide,*
where he showed himself over 40 years to be one of the finest
proponents of a comic tradition which began with Twain and
extended to Benchley and Ring Lardner.

Now in his late sixties ("and in a place with a 13-year lease: draw
your own conclusion about the chances they give me") Perelman
has just published *Baby, It's Cold Inside,* a collection of stories
which show that the old buffer is still crystal sharp. The essence
of his unique and durable style, apparently, lay in rough blending.
He explains the alchemy thus:

"As a writer, I've read all the worst that has been thought and
said by man. I practically blinded myself throughout youth by

reading all the trash that's ever been written, mingled with an
education in Greek and Latin, the results of which were dubious.
Anyway, it all formed kind of a mash. I went to waterfront dives to
see skinflicks made for sailors—*Sex Maniac* is one of the best
films I ever saw—and I immersed myself in cheap magazines like
Adventure and *Black Mask* where, incidentally, both Sam Spade
and Philip Marlowe were created. Fowler, in *English Usage,* would
refer to the resultant prose style as the bower bird variety, which
is to say it contained an ostentatious display of learning. But then,
Sir Thomas Browne and a lot of others did it before me, so I
guess I'm not all that apologetic.''

In the Footsteps of Phileas Fogg

Mary Blume / 1971

As appeared in the *International Herald Tribune* 30 January 1971. Reprinted by permission of Mary Blume.

'He was ever the same impassive gentleman, the imperturbable member of the Reform Club, upon whom no incident could come as a surprise.'
　　—JULES VERNE, *'Around the World in Eighty Days.'*

PARIS.—Verne's description of Phileas Fogg applies equally to another imperturbable member of the Reform Club in Pall Mall, the svelte American writer S. J. Perelman.

In March Mr. Perelman will leave London and, emulating Fogg, will try to girdle the globe in only 80 days.

Like Fogg, Mr. Perelman will travel by liner, railway, carriage, yacht, trading vessel, sledge and elephant. He will not set foot on an airplane, possibly from fear of being delayed. As far as possible he will follow Fogg's itinerary from London to Suez to Bombay to Calcutta to Hong Kong to Yokohama to San Francisco to New York to London.

"I am up to my well-known hips in making arrangements," said Mr. Perelman while reconnoitering recently in Paris. An intrepid traveler, he tracked down Dracula's castle in Romania, was in Kenya during the Mau-Mau revolt and bought a sports car once in Bangkok. He currently lives in Kensington in London.

Instead of playing whist like Fogg, Mr. Perelman will while away the voyage typing up his adventures for *The New Yorker*. The articles will come out in book form, illustrated by Ronald Searle, in 1972 to celebrate the 100th anniversary of Fogg's trip.

Mr. Perelman plans to write a running critique on Verne, noting inaccuracies as he goes along (a mistake in Verne's description of the Reform Club roof has led Mr. Perelman to doubt that he ever visited London).

Mr. Perelman will himself commit a great inaccuracy: using the

most specious reasoning, he claims that if Verne were writing
today he would give Fogg a girl companion instead of the manser-
vant Passepartout. From a long list of applicants, Mr. Perelman
has selected Dianne Baker, his dishy secretary, to be his Passepar-
toute.

The arrangements are so complicated that they have been put
into the hands of a travel agent, Mr. Le Bas, an unflappable pint-
sized gentleman with sparkling eyes. Mr. Le Bas was so inflamed
by Mr. Perelman's project that he re-read *Around the World in 80
Days* under his bedclothes by candlelight during the English power
cut. He says that Mr. Perelman's trip will be harder than Fogg's
because there are fewer cargo ships these days and many of them
are containerized and passengerless.

The worst part of the trip, caused by the closing of the Suez
Canal, forces Mr. Perelman to make a long detour via Bari, Haifa
and Elat, where he will catch a boat to Bombay.

"This is made necessary," Mr. Perelman explained, "because
the canal is full of old rubber bands and unshaven, disgruntled
seamen playing cards on those rusting hulks."

As a writer of Mike Todd's film version of *Around the World in
80 Days,* Mr. Perelman is in possession of the actual hat David
Niven wore from Suez to Bombay.

Along with assorted dentists, lawyers and other Todd cronies, he
also has Fogg's original carpet bag, of which Todd had 100
examples made.

"Once and for all, you must squelch the idea that there is a
balloon in the book," Mr. Perelman said. "Todd heisted that from
Verne's *Five Weeks in a Balloon.*"

If there is no balloon, there is an elephant which Mr. Perelman
must ride in India, rescuing a handsome widow from a suttee
along the way. The Indian Tourist Office in London is helping to
locate an elephant and several London ladies have volunteered to
play the rescued widow and repose upon the suttee.

"The best-looking one is Linda Lewis, Tony Lewis's wife, but as
I pointed out to her, she is so tall that it would require an
oversized suttee and I don't know if I can afford it.

"Should her eye fall on this," Mr. Perelman added, "the other two birds weren't bad-looking either, so she shouldn't get a swelled head.''

After rescuing the widow Mr. Perelman will have a restful 22 days crossing the Pacific. "It should be a lot better when we get out of India," he pointed out. "But then it's always better when you get out of India."

Mr. Perelman's plans have gladdened the hearts of ship captains, shiny-suited agents who figure there must be a fast buck to be made on it somehow, editors, civil and military tailors, mahouts and bookies (bets are being placed on his chances of completing the voyage, just as they were on Fogg's). What has been the reaction at the Reform Club?

"It's hard to say. They've been pretty impassive so far."

Leaving 15 minutes later than Fogg, Mr. Perelman plans to depart from the steps of the Reform Club at 9 p.m., heading for the Channel ferry, Calais, Paris and the Rome Express. Exactly 80 days later, he intends to present himself again at the Reform Club and state with sublime cool, as Fogg did, "Here I am, gentlemen."

"It will be very funny," Mr. Perelman said, "if no one's there."

Words and Their Masters

Israel Shenker / 1974

From *Words and Their Masters* by Israel Shenker. Doubleday. New York. 1974:17–20, 201–5, 364–8. Reprinted by permission of Israel Shenker.

S. J. Perelman–I

In a display of courage beyond the pall of duty, S. J. Perelman arrived in New York the other day.

The other day? Today? The days blur into a clammy, polluted mess when the humorist thinks of Fun City.

"Obviously, Mayor Lindsay was being ironical when he called it Fun City," said Mr. Perelman, failingly elegant in checked shirt and fevered brow. Mopping the perspiration from that brow, he added: "I would call it something else, except the Bible has beaten me to the punch. Sodom and Gomorrah. Unfortunately, all the good words have been coined."

During the best part of the year Mr. Perelman's home was a farm in Pennsylvania's Bucks County, sixty-four miles as the smog lies from his Sodom and Gomorrah. There he was tapping out an autobiography, and the reliving was not easy.

"I'd just reached the part where I graduate from nursery school with blazing honors," he said.

The work would tell almost all of what he did to rise from the fiery peak to the punnacle from which he tosses off—bleeding with every syllable—unparalleled, not to say oblique, looks at the obscure perils of the age. Most of his humor falls into the pages of *The New Yorker,* for subsequent enshrinement in book collections with such hinting titles as *The Rising Gorge, Acres and Pains, Chicken Inspector #23* and *The Road to Miltown or Under the Spreading Atrophy.*

His autobiography-in-halting-progress was as yet untitled. "It was always safe to ask [John] O'Hara the title of his next," Mr. Perelman said, "because it was already out. But I'm a practicing writer."

Preparing for the ordeal of a visit to New York, he recalled, "I confined myself for two days to a closet without any air holes and I turned on the radio full blast; I got into as many claustrophobic situations as I could around the house."

From the dreaded moment of arrival "I saw 10 million damply moist faces showing the mingled hostility and depression that typifies every New York resident. It was like a day in Los Angeles, which resembles a gigantic steam laundry, and you are employed leaning over a tub of damp laundry."

"I think everybody here is *ferrikt* [*meshugga*]," said Mr. Perelman, "which is a dangerous state of mind. I think the city pulsates with insanity. Only last week a lady was standing at a newsstand and a man drove a knife into her stomach. Eventually people noticed that she was lying there bleeding to death.

"I was almost annihilated by the chauffeur of a Fleetwood sedan—a juggernaut. I was trying to cross Sixth Avenue and he practically clipped me at the knee and hamstrung me. He shrieked an obscenity at me, and my reply was inaudible since he was accelerating.

"And of course if you own a car and have a *jimjick* that doesn't work, the next voice you hear is the voice of the mechanic saying, 'That'll be $42.50.' "

"It's become a way of life," he insisted. "If you are compelled to be a resident, you walk around figuratively with your fist doubled. When you get onto a New York bus you must be booted and spurred, ready for the attack of the driver. It's a reflex you have to develop.

"Things are even worse in the department stores—which I abominate. There's a hierarchy of oppression—the smallest stockroom boy is the victim of the saleslady who's dominated by the floor-walker who's oppressed by the floor manager. Last week I read about a sale where women bit each other. Emile Zola is the only writer I know of who wrote about department-store tyranny. It was life imitating art."

Before he avoided the department stores, Mr. Perelman felt obliged to check in at his hostilery. "The moment I stepped into the hotel," he said, "I questioned a mysterious rise in price for the room.

" 'Everything's gone up $2,' the man barked. Bang. Immediately my head rolled in the sand."

Meals were hardly less fatal. "In New York restaurants you have to swallow the scorn of the waiter and the maître d', and you have to be humbly grateful even if you're served the wrong food. There should be a Michelin Guide which would award three harpoons to restaurants for rudeness. Gradually you become whipped and you slink out to the native heath, where the only things you can revenge yourself on are the dogs and the wife."

He went on: "New Yorkers are very proud of their city. I really don't know why. There was a time when it was bearable. When this was a city of six million—although it was a termitary, a home for termites—it still was possible. The addition of four million people and the millions who come in from outside to work here have made the city impossible.

"When you approach it you see—not a mushroom cloud as yet—but a pall that hangs over the city. I felt I was becoming too healthy in the country, and I thought I needed to have a few whiffs of carbon monoxide to tone up my system."

"I think it's a city now for people who are under twenty-five—possibly twenty-eight," he said. "I don't think anybody over twenty-eight has the stamina to live here. It's the lodestone? lodestone?—I always mix them up—of those who are not fortunate enough to be in a line of work that permits them to be somewhere else."

Mr. Perelman comes but once a month, driven to the extremity by the demands of the market for his prose.

"There are a lot of clichés about the city—you have the theater and the museums. Most of these things are available to you outside New York.

"On the other hand, if you're a fancier of aggression and hostility, you find the outstanding examples here. If you are a student psychiatrist you should come here because you'll find a wider degree of neuroses, mental imbalance and *narrishkeit* [*meshugga-ness*] than you'll find in the country."

Watching over the traffic are New York City's finest. "Yes," agreed Mr. Perelman, "the blue coats are still my favorites—sturdy boys in blue. But I wouldn't have any contact with them,

normally, except to slip a cube of poisoned sugar to a policeman's horse."

Is there no way to fight? "Study cringing and humility," Mr.
Perelman replied. "It's also possible that science may evolve a
drug that would change the victim into the aggressor. But I think
the ordinary New York citizen is fated to be a Kafka character. He's
constantly on trial for something the nature of which he doesn't
understand."

Leaving New York is no less perilous an exercise than getting
here. "If you emerge too suddenly," Mr. Perelman warns,
"you're likely to get the bends, like a sandhog coming up from the
East River. You have to go to a place like the Paramus Shopping
Center and adjust slowly to the quiet."

S. J. Perelman–II

Had you pattered past the sleeper in New York's Century Club
recently, you might have glimpsed a recumbent figure, half
shrouded by the gloom, resembling a startled yawn. In peccable
tweed and shirt of many colors, mustache limp and granny glasses
clouded, he waved tentatively as you approached.

Stiffening toward the vertical with an agility belying his studied
air of languor, he was suddenly the sitting image of a famous and
debonair author named S. J. Perelman—the very same who once
cut a fashionable swath through the most ethereal literary reaches
of Providence, Rhode Island, and County Bucks, Pennsylvania.

Hardly a year before this Perelman had left his native heath,
scattering maledictions on the tribe of Gotham, muttering impre-
cations from the collected apocrypha of Sodom the Magnificent,
and swearing curses stolen *in toto* from the deathbed scene of the
Morte d'Arthur. He had taken refuge in furnished digs in London's
Onslow Gardens, a fashionable corner which had earlier given
refuge to the no-less-distinguished man of initial letters, P. G.
Wodehouse. (There is something about Onslow—a *je ne sais quoi* of
enforced abandon—which attracts authors reduced to the genteel
poverty of initials.)

"It is hardly seventy days since I left London, but it seems

years," said this Perelman of purest ray serene, who had been
shlepping himself around the world following the itinerary of Phileas
Fogg in Jules Verne's *Around the World in 80 Days.* At the end of
the trail he would write an account of his adventures and reveal the
worst about the fleshpots of Araby and the retreads of Nineveh
and Tyre. It was the least he could do to keep his literary agent in
accustomed splendor.

Thanks to advice from the Ouija board, his course had swerved a
smidgeon. "I am a great believer in the infallibility of the Ouija
board," said the Fogg-bound author, "and I have used it to commu-
nicate with the departed spirits of Ring Lardner, Scott Fitzgerald,
Robert Benchley, and Alexander Woollcott.

"In Fitzgerald's case, the answers were in two styles, which was
only appropriate: Fitzgerald wrote junk for the *Saturday Evening
Post,* and higher artistic style in his books. In Benchley's and
Lardner's case, the replies were funny. Woollcott's answers were
bitchy, and that was expectable."

Consulted about Verne, the Ouija boards spelled out a destination. "Go to deli," it said. Ouija boards are now plastic rather
than teak, and they lose something in translation. Instead of pro-
ceeding directly to Bloom's delicatessen in the East End (of London),
Perelman assumed the plastic was nattering in Litvak and meant
"Delhi." He therefore reoriented himself and—though India is
not his favorite gem of the East—detoured there to see what the
Ouija wanted from his occidental *neshuma* (soul).

What he found was a myna bird, scion of an ancient mynasty,
and Perelman christened it "Nixon's Vulture." The myna is now
devoted to him, and wherever Perelman goes the bird is sure to go;
it followed him to shul one day. Asked to identify the sex of his
bird, Perelman said: "If he or she lays an egg, we have a clue, but
until then we're in the dark. I think he's trying to say her name, but
this may be only paternal pride."

From Delhi the course of empire lay east across the waves,
aboard a P. & O. liner peopled with people by Somerset Maugham
and decked out with deckhands by Joseph Conrad. "But in Hong
Kong, Singapore, and Tokyo I ran into a great many blue-headed
American ladies," said Perelman, shaking the ashes from his El
Ruducto. "These blue-headed gorgons buy themselves countless

formals and then it's a dress parade all across the Pacific. They talk very loudly, clearly, insistently, and peremptorily. There's a good deal of drinking, to which I certainly don't object, except it makes their talk even more articulate and vocal."

Perelman continued: "So I took a 747, and from where I was sitting I could watch both the movies at once. One film had Ursula Andress and some *boychik* in a spy thing, and in the fourth or fifth reel, just as they got into bed together without benefit of covering, the couple in the other film shucked their clothes and got naked.

"Apparently in the fourth or fifth reel of films now it's mandatory to take off your clothes and have carnal knowledge of each other. I put the cover over the myna bird while I went on trying to figure out what was happening."

The author sifted through American customs at Honolulu, which he called "the most three-words-missing-here frontier in the world."* Continuing to bowdlerize, he recalled the scene: "Forty people, babies crying, and this beetle-browed customs inspector, with little eyes like gimlets, opens everybody's baggage, pulling aside the hairpins, obviously searching for pot while pigeons fly overhead, their wings beating against the sky, their undercarriages laden with pot and morphine."

California lay ahead. "They're sunk in apathy and despair," he said of the citizenry. "A lot of houses are for sale in Beverly Hills, and the great arteries still lead nowhere except to the imagination of Saul Steinberg. Nobody's in the luxury shops except a few women, dressed to the teeth, usually in pants—the teeth have little sweaters on them.

"I remember when there were only nineteen banks on Wilshire between Santa Monica Boulevard and La Brea. Now there are seventy-six. In London the banks look like groceries, and the bank managers give you overdrafts. Here the banks look like courthouses and the bank manager has flinty eyes, a square face, and phony good humor radiating from his visage. But the teeth become a steel trap as soon as there's a question of borrowing a few dinero."

Grinding his cigar into an ash tray rushed to the scene by a gentleman in waiting, Perelman peered about this lair of anger and steeled his sword arm for the *pièce de résistance*—New York. "I can sum it up in one word—*geferlech*," he said. "When I saw those filthy newspapers blowing up 45th Street I realized this is a disaster area—all the streets are. It's tawdry and filthy, and the streets are pitted, just the way the snow left them winter before last. I bounced in from Kennedy over craters like the moon."

"You know those lines from 'The Star-Spangled Banner'?" he went on, " '. . . the rocket's red glare, the bombs bursting in air'? It's all apropos now. Francis Scott Key had a certain amount of prevision."

Drawing closer, Mr. Perelman whispered a confidence. He had brought with him a secret weapon against the terrors of his native soil: "Malice—sheer, adulterated malice."

Suffering from his attack of British understatement, Mr. Perelman had earlier gone off to see his family physician, an eminent practitioner who made his last house call in 1929, and can still recite the circumstances.

"My name is Sidney Mountain Perelman, and I have come to see Mohammed," the patient told the receptionist.

The gainly wench looked up from the money bag she was fondling and inspected the quivering patient. Perelman had been dreading this moment, and had spent the previous fortnight flexing his knee in preparation for the physician's knock. "When he finishes tapping me with hammers, I'm fit for *gurnisht,*" the author confessed.

But the doctor said Perelman was in fine shape. "This is what they always say," commented Perelman, "and then the next thing you hear is: 'Celebrated author keels over on the *Queen Elizabeth* while playing shuffleboard—a case of marine cardiac arrest.' "

And yet he could hardly wait to get back to London, where he had won fame as the man who rubs Ouijas with Princess Margaret and shares the inscrutable wisdom of the East with American Ambassador Walter H. Annenberg: "I told him that if the pepper-seed takes root it will leave a dragon fly."

His Excellency replied that latterly his own interest had been swerving to oriental sculpture, subject to the discomfiture caused by elements of refurbishing and rehabilitation.

Discomfiture in London agreed with Perelman. "You have to adapt yourself to living with cold, wet feet," he said, "and sunshine never bothers you."

Raising himself from the couch, he apologized that he had to get
back aboard the *QE* II to get the links out of his shuffleboard, to pour
champagne for friends come to see him off, and to feed his bird.
"The little swine would eat all day," said Perelman, running into
traffic with one arm flexed defensively, his knees jerking convul-
sively, his noble front knit in wrath. The author disappeared from
sight, a man of infinite custom whom rage has not withered.

S. J. Perelman–III

S. J. Perelman, the man without a country home, has returned to
his native New York City.

"English life, while very pleasant, is rather bland," he said. "I
expected kindness and gentility, and I found it, but there is such
a thing as too much couth.

"There rye bread has no caraway seeds, and their name for
corned beef is salt beef—and it doesn't compare with what you
can get on the Upper West Side or on the Lower East Side."

When he left these shores, two years earlier, his appetites for the
pleasures of Gotham were sated, and he was dimly perceived to
be uttering a plague on all its houses.

"New York was then—and it still obviously is—a very difficult
place for anyone to be," he said. "When you first return, the city
seems very distressing, and all the things we know about New York
are true—the dirt, the disorder, the violence. But I find myself
adapting: I walk on the balls of my feet at night.

"Having been born here, I guess I wouldn't want to renounce my
birthright. Perhaps, just barely perhaps, it's necessary to go somewhere else to get a view of one's city.

"When I'm away, I miss the tension, the give and take. I feel it's
a great mistake for any writer to cut himself off from his roots. One's
work suffers by trying to transplant it to another milieu.

"My style is mélange—a mixture of all the sludge I read as a
child, all the clichés, liberal doses of Yiddish, criminal slang, and
some of what I was taught in a Providence, Rhode Island, school
by impatient teachers. When I tried to think of an idiomatic expression
in London, I had to reach for it. I felt out of touch with the idiom."

And he suffered the pangs of sloth: "Have you ever gone to a doctor to have him remove your sloth?"

He was actually on his way there to see about a swollen toe. "Last night I heard the call of the muse and I got out of bed in the dark and kicked a rocking chair," he explained. "I'm afraid the toe may be broken. Next time I'll light the way with flares.

"I don't normally rush to the typewriter. Any writer who tells you he's in a hurry to get to that desk is a faker, not a writer, but I feel quite revitalized by being in New York."

His best friends live in or near this city; not far from his East Side sublet is a bakery with seeds in the rye; he found an affable Chinese laundryman; and there is a discount drugstore. "What more do I need?" he demanded.

"I never made any promise not to come back or to become an expatriate," he said. "I don't even like the word.

"The rest of America I have always liked very much. I love New England, I love the countryside, I revisited the Bucks County farm where I lived forty years."

Whenever he goes, he carries his London *Sunday Times* press card, which bears a warning that "it must be surrendered to the Foreign Editor on demand."

Mr. Perelman has a recurring nightmare in which the editor seizes him by the epaulets and strips him of his credentials, as well as his corncob pipe and his copy of the *American Mercury*—which were standard reportorial tools in the days of H. L. Mencken.

"In my waking hours in London I saw myself as Joel McCrea in *Foreign Correspondent,* wearing a double-breasted trench coat and hiding in windmills," he said. "I finally realized I was Perelman from Providence, Rhode Island.

"I've never tried to use the press card in this country, because I'm sure it would get me into the Tombs as an impostor or into Watergate as an electrician.

"What's going on with this Administration reminds me of Warren Harding and the Teapot Dome, and we should all be bathed in shame about what went on in Vietnam."

When Mr. Perelman returned to claim his share of the Gross National Product, he came aboard the *France,* and, to avoid wrinkling his cummerbund, he went Tourist. "I was told it was just as good as First Class," he said. "I can nail that lie immediately.

"When I got back to this country, I was treated as I would expect Meyer Lansky to be treated. Eventually I was escorted to a taxi. When I got to my destination, the clock showed $2.75. I prepared to give the taxi driver a dollar tip. He emitted a cry which began 'I waited all day for this ship to come in . . .' A whole *megilla* [song and dance]. So I paid him an extra $2.75, and I slunk off feeling like a hayseed or a rhubarb—I hate to remember which."

Mr. Perelman still recalls "marked contrasts" between New York and London. When he told a London taxi driver "I'm terribly late for an appointment in the city," the fellow said equably, "We'll try."

"Had a similar thing happened, beginning at Madison and Fifty-second," Mr. Perelman suggested, "the taxi driver would have said, 'What do you think I am? A goddamn genius? Look at that traffic!' "

In relaxed London moments, Mr. Perelman would set out afoot with his shopping bag to buy one orange, a tin of sardines, and one napoleon for dessert. "In the shops I'd meet the aged widows of British India officers, with straight backs, living in straitened circumstances," he said. "They would each buy one small object—an orange, a tin of sardines, one napoleon for dessert."

He misses them, and he misses the police as well. "Britain's men in blue are still mannerly," he noted. "How corruptible they are I can't say. Occasionally you hear a story about a British policeman caught accepting an orange."

"It's a pleasure to listen to tales of erring-do on the non-commercial radio while shaving in London," Mr. Perelman said.

"That happens to be the most creative period of my day—the contact of the blade with the cheek stimulates the creative process. The thoughts are chiefly lubricious."

The more he shaves the more pleasant his recollections of London. "What I would like to do hereafter is spend my winters in New York, and three or four months of each summer in England," he said. "That still leaves the spring and autumn unaccounted for, and maybe then I can let my beard grow and become the castaway God intended me to be."

*Reprinted as in original

S. J. Perelman—He's America's Lampoonist Laureate

Maralyn Lois Polak / 1975

From *The Writer as Celebrity* by Maralyn Lois Polak, 30 March 1975. Copyright © 1986 Maralyn Lois Polak. Reprinted by permission of M. Evans and Company, Inc.

"I think humor in America has greatly declined and may disappear entirely," growls S. J. Perelman. Seated in a black leather chair, his feet by the radiator, he suggests, "It is not easy to satirize the absurd when the absurd has become official."

S. J. Perelman gives pomposity a good name. Give him a cliché and he takes a mile. *The New York Times,* which must know, labeled him "America's lampoonist laureate," and he's been variously dubbed "a satirical wielder of the acid pen," "one of today's greatest nonsense writers," "terrifyingly jocose." The titles of his pieces bear truest witness to his screwball wit. To wit: *A Child's Garden of Curses, The Ill-Tempered Clavichord, Road to Miltown, Malice in Wonderland, Acres and Pains, Chicken Inspector #23.*

The humor is missing today.

He does not want his conversation to be recorded, and he is not exactly overjoyed at being interviewed. He would have much preferred to continue affixing sticky tape to large cardboard cartons containing his possessions, so he could leave shortly on yet another globe-girdling journey to whet yet another book.

A cranky, erudite septuagenarian, Sidney Joseph Perelman wears a neat clipped mustache and the same oval steel-rimmed glasses he picked up in Paris in 1927. After selling his Bucks County retreat four years ago, resettling in London as a much-heralded "resident alien," then moving back to his loved/hated New York, he lives momentarily in a quietly elegant Manhattan hotel overlooking Gramercy Park. Soft-spoken though nasal, with a courtly command of exotic English, he is a small man seemingly surrounded by eyebrows. His red plaid shirt is probably a relic from his pastoral past.

The celebrated humorist and author of countless high-gloss, high-brow-comic *New Yorker* essays, books, films, and plays, does not seem to be in good humor. Owlishly doleful, he does not particularly care to discuss pretty girls, despite his reputation as a literary Lothario. He does not care to discuss dirty jokes, though he is considered a connoisseur of the genre. He does not care to discuss the Marx Brothers, for whom he ghosted gags during their *Horse Feathers* daze.

He describes his meticulously crafted writing style as "a mixture of all the trash I read as a child, all the clichés, criminal slang, liberal doses of Yiddish, and some of what I learned in school from impatient teachers.

"I have all the neuroses and prejudices we collect as we get older. I think spoken English is becoming corrupted, but that's nothing new," he humphs, and I decide to say only yes and no for the duration. "Current writing isn't too distinguished. By strict definition, a writer should be a reader. Young writers don't read enough these days." Before I can rush to the defense, he reminisces.

"On Fridays, growing up, I'd go to the Providence, Rhode Island, library and take out eleven books and spend the weekend sitting in the kitchen, my feet in the oven, munching cookies and reading trash." Trash? "That's right," he nods. "Adventures, detectives, romance. They help fertilize the brain, like mulch.

"I had been drawing pictures from infancy and wanted to be a cartoonist. I even drew cartoons in my father's drygoods store on the long cardboard strips around which the bolts of cotton were stored," he says. "After college I became a comic artist for some humor magazines. I'd write jokes that had nothing to do with my pictures, an intricate system of verbiage, founded on puns like 'I have Bright's disease, and he has mine!' Soon the captions of my drawings"—curiously morbid woodcuts—"got longer and longer. Finally they displaced the drawings entirely."

He's been a free-lance writer for fifty years. "Call it a license to starve," he jests. "But I work very slowly. I'm a bleeder. It's a good day when I get a page done. I think easy writing makes hard reading. Actually I find writing a very time-consuming, painful process. And when anyone introduces me as a humorist, I get

somewhat nervous. There's something about the term that is a bit
off-putting.

"Humor meant to be read—humorous writing—is passing out of
existence. As a class this sort of writer is doomed. A person so
impelled today usually ends up as part of a six-man joke-writing
team."

Or in Hollywood. "The dream factory," he says with a flourish
of his cigarette. "Hollywood is a dreary industrial town controlled
by hoodlums of enormous wealth. I worked for all kinds of weird
people. My late wife and I collaborated during the thirties. The
studios had a profound respect for husband-and-wife teams, thought
they were fashionable. They were under the impression they'd
get double value—writing during the day, discussing the script in
bed at night."

In 1957 S. J. Perelman received an Oscar for his screenplay of
Mike Todd's epic extravaganza *Around the World in 80 Days*. Did
he reject the "bourgeois bauble"? No. "I think everyone who
receives an Oscar, even myself, is delighted. All those excited gur-
glings and gushes you see on the TV box were hardly what I felt,
but I was pleased," he concedes gruffly.

"For some time I used my Oscar as a doorstop. When I tired of
that I stored it in a drawer and forgot I had it. Each time I've opened
the drawer, I have a sense of wonder and discovery anew." He
grins. "You know, it would make a good weapon to protect
oneself from muggers, though a bit heavy to carry around the
streets of New York as a steady form of defense.

"I've lived in a number of places in my life and can't make up my
mind which is the most agreeable. I enjoy travel so much, but I
find most places after a lengthy stay turn out to have drawbacks.
So"—he peers at me with his watery blue eyes—"the idea is to
be a moving target. Then it's impossible for people to pick you off.
But the Delaware Valley is really one of the loveliest sections in
the world. After my wife died, I sold the hundred-acre farm in
Erwinna, where we had lived for forty years, and went to London.
Too much rural splendor—Bucks County summers were hot as
Bangkok.

"So your next question automatically will be why did I leave
England after saying I was there in perpetuity? I did stay for three

years. But it wasn't favorable for my work. Too much gentility, civility, couth. Nothing at which to get irritated. Besides, the British never heard of bagels, definitely a flaw in their character.

"Actually I get quite homesick for Bucks. I keep an elderly, very cute MG stored in a barn there, perhaps as a subconscious pledge that I'll return. Occasionally I do visit," he admits. "I wrap my arms about the fenders and sob lovingly, causing the chrome to become rusty. But I definitely need New York for my work. It's detestable, dangerous, filthy—the city, I mean—corroding, more and more pestilential, twice-breathed air, and all. But there's a feeling of pulse around me. Everyone is busy. That's inspiring."

S. J. Perelman's thirst for geographic novelty and stimulating literary material has taken him on African safaris, in search of illicit sturgeon, and around the world in eighty days—shades of Jules Verne—by steamship, train, and lady elephant. "I was duplicating the exploits of Phileas Fogg one hundred years after Verne's fantasy. The trip was remarkably without incident," he says, shrugging. "We crossed the southern part of India by elephant. Highly uncomfortable. Though the elephant was dressed in very feminine garb—gilded tusks, ankle bells, pendant earrings, a little silver cap. She was very sweet, but . . ." Not his type.

The experience provoked several essays that eventually found their way into Perelman's latest book, *Vinegar Puss,* a title whose unfortunate origins I had been unwilling to speculate upon. All right, S. J., I do not want to ask this, but I must. Any relation between you and the title? "It's an old expression," he explains patiently, "equivalent to sourpuss. Which is what I evolved after looking at a publicity photograph of myself.

"But I don't really see myself that way," S. J. Perelman disclaims. "Actually, I'm a fun-loving, sunny-tempered fellow," He chuckles. "I don't know what my enemies think."

Interview with S. J. Perelman

Dick Cavett / 1977

From *The Dick Cavett Show*, 29 November 1977 Guest: S. J.
Perelman. Published by permission of Daphne Productions.

Dick Cavett: Good evening. My guest tonight, S. J. Perelman,
doesn't mind being described as a crank. He has described himself
in that manner. However, I think it's better and probably more
accurate to describe him as Eudora Welty did, as a living national
treasure. One of America's great humorists, S. J. Perelman.

Mr. Perelman, I apologize in advance for the fact that I will
occasionally pronounce your name Pearlman, in the ensuing half
hour, because I was raised to pronounce it wrong. Groucho always
pronounced it Pearlman and then I tried a nmemonic device,
which was to remember *The Perils of Pauline,* but that hasn't
worked because it was played by Pearl White and so, I realized
that's why I'm back where I started. Can you forgive me?

S. J. Perelman: I can, but I'm absolutely anesthetic to this whole
matter. I've been called that and worse.

Dick Cavett: So, we can muddle through, I hope.

S. J. Perelman: I hope so, yes.

Dick Cavett: The last time I saw you, you had escaped America
to get away from some of its uncouth aspects. Then I saw you,
again, when you had come back from England, where you found an
excess of couth. I hope the —to quote you, cycle hasn't come
around again. Are you feeling like leaving again or are you here
to stay?

S. J. Perelman: No. I leave with some regularity. I get away once
or twice a year to England just sort of to charge my batteries.
And on the whole, this is where I function best or worst. So, for the
time being, that's the picture.

Dick Cavett: I've found that Ireland has become fashionable for
certain members of the smart-set, the movie-set, the literary-set,
to buy second or third homes in. Has that ever appealed to you?

S. J. Perelman: In point of fact, I was over there this summer looking around for a small pad, small Georgian pad with about thirty rooms.

Dick Cavett: With a lot of spread.

S. J. Perelman: Yes, something that a man can roll up his sleeves in. It is. It's a wonderful part of Ireland. I have never seen the country around Cork. Have you been down there?

Dick Cavett: No, I've only seen it in the John Ford films.

S. J. Perelman: Well, it's been heavily exploited there, I agree, but it's a very pretty part of Ireland and I could well ride up there for a spell. It's very green and . . .

Dick Cavett: It looks enchanting.

S. J. Perelman: Yes.

Dick Cavett: To coin a phrase.

S. J. Perelman: Yes.

Dick Cavett: Traveling has multiple veins for you. One of the things in *Eastward Ha!* which is a travel book in some sense, is the problem of the laundry. It seems to pile up when you travel and it's never been solved.

S. J. Perelman: No, it hasn't really, not for me. There's nothing as dis-spiriting as opening your suitcase and having a gusher of laundry bubble up, you know, and I usually know that it's time to stop, at least global travel, when that happens.

Dick Cavett: Drip-dry hasn't solved this problem, then.

S. J. Perelman: No, not really, because have you ever worn a drip-dry shirt? You know, it really is a combination of plaster-board and saw-tooth. It absolutely cuts your neck to ribbons partic-ularly in a hot climate.

Dick Cavett: Yes, but at least it's dry.

S. J. Perelman: It is dry.

Dick Cavett: You can air a *shaphalee* in it.

S. J. Perelman: Dry and miserable.

Dick Cavett: If you can solve the laundry problem, would you travel more? It would be hard to imagine how you couldn't travel more. You've been everywhere, Phineas Fog.

S. J. Perelman: Phileas, please.

Dick Cavett: Phileas. Did I say Phineas?

S. J. Perelman: You said Phineas.

Dick Cavett: All right, I'm terribly sorry. I lose a point on that.

S. J. Perelman: I'll report you.

Dick Cavett: I am blushing.

S. J. Perelman: No, I think I've had the long around-the-world circuit.

Dick Cavett: Yeah.

S. J. Perelman: I've done it six or seven times and it's becoming a little familiar. I haven't been in South America at all.

Dick Cavett: Any particular prejudice there?

S. J. Perelman: I can't say. I've often gotten myself into a corner and asked why this was. I suppose I still tend to think of it as a collection of banana republics. And while I'm highly sympathetic to their woes and all that sort of thing, there's so much political trouble there now anyhow, it would be a difficult place to travel in.

Dick Cavett: Maybe not meat for the comic mill or grist for the mill or meat for the mill is a badly mixed metaphor, isn't it. I just lost another point.

S. J. Perelman: How far down are you?

Dick Cavett: I'm near the back of the class, already, I can see that. Say, speaking of class, if you were hired by a university, could they conceivably afford you, which is ludicrous, to teach a course in writing and comic writing, in particularly, would you give back the ticket?

S. J. Perelman: Yes, I think I would because I don't think you can teach it. I think there are some people who have an aptitude or sense of fun or perhaps an innate gaiety of some kind. My friend William Zinsser is up at Yale now and he has been trying an experiment of that sort. I haven't seen him recently, so I don't know how it's coming along, but he has tried to get people to write comic things and it's questionable whether it can be done.

Dick Cavett: My guess is that perhaps you could improve someone who has a gift, but I don't think you could impart the gift, obviously.

S. J. Perelman: Well, I think the whole process starts really at a much younger age, and it's compounded of interest in reading and a willingness to imitate.

Dick Cavett: Really? To imitate.

S. J. Perelman: Yes, because I know that the first comic writer I ever remember reading was Stephen Leacock, the Canadian writer,

and subsequently George Ade and Ring Lardner, of course. I was
such a shameless Lardner thief that I should have been arrested,
really. The editors who bought my work at that time either were not
aware of Lardner's work, but I pillaged him unmercifully.

Dick Cavett: I think it's brave of you to admit that. Are you likely
to get a bill from the Lardner estate for this confession?

S. J. Perelman: Well, if Ring Lardner, Jr. is listening, I owe him
a lot of money. But also Mencken. There was a big Mencken period
when I was so influenced by Mencken—this was sort of at the end
of college. I think that any writer who says he is not influenced
by the work of contemporaries or people in the past is really dis-
honest.

Dick Cavett: Can you think of anyone who is an exception to
that—who is a total original? Who just has no predecessors at all in
style, form?

S. J. Perelman: No, but I can tell you that . . .

Dick Cavett: James Joyce, maybe.

S. J. Perelman: Well, even Joyce. For example, do you know the
famous Lodcraft poster called, "The Devon Choponea."

Dick Cavett: I happen to know that.

S. J. Perelman: With what's-her-name in the center, the lady.

Dick Cavett: The lady, I always . . .

S. J. Perelman: Now, the man bending over her shoulder with
the yellow beard. Do you recollect that there is a man?

Dick Cavett: Is it Joyce?

S. J. Perelman: No, but that is a French writer, from whom Joyce
took the whole conception of the interior monologue, the stream
of consciousness.

Dick Cavett: Really?

S. J. Perelman: Yes. It appeared in a book called—to translate,
it's a French title, "The Laurels Are Cut Down." Oh, yes, his name
was Edward Duchadan, the author.

Dick Cavett: Duchadan.

S. J. Perelman: And he is the man standing over this lady.

Dick Cavett: That's fascinating, anyway.

S. J. Perelman: And Joyce acknowledged his indebtedness to
Duchadan. So, obviously, everybody's been influenced.

Dick Cavett: Have you seen your influence grow in other writers?

S. J. Perelman: Well, I've read reviewers and critics commenting on books of mine and there seems to be some sort of a compulsion to write. And what they say is my style, but I think that anyone who writes like us or comic stuff, suffers from that. Ogden Nash, for example—whenever Ogden's books came out, invariably, a child's plural on the times, all kinds of people try to review him in the manner, you know . . .

Dick Cavett: Yes, I can understand that because I find myself tending to speak differently around you because one is so aware of language with you, but to me that's like imitating—meeting Groucho and imitating Groucho to his face or something. People used to do that. I can't imagine. You can imagine what he said and thought about them. Did you turn Groucho onto Leacock or—is it pronounced Leacock? He's one of my favorite writers.

S. J. Perelman: Oh, he's marvelous.

Dick Cavett: You can still find his books in secondhand stores, only. I think he must be almost totally out of print, is he?

S. J. Perelman: Yes. And . . .

Dick Cavett: Groucho liked him very much. I wondered if you have influenced Groucho there.

S. J. Perelman: Well, I would think that Groucho must have discovered him before we ever met. But Groucho was a great admirer of Abe Martin. Do you know . . .

Dick Cavett: Abe Martin? No.

S. J. Perelman: He was a famous Indiana humorist and also artist. And Groucho used to go around quoting him. He lived in Brown County, Indiana, and he did little drawings, just a tiny thing with just one line underneath, which was usually a witty characterization of people in Brown County. And his work is still to be found in secondhand shops. Groucho was mad about him.

Dick Cavett: I'm going to look him up.

S. J. Perelman: Yes, you must. His real name was Ken Hubbard, but he wrote under the name of Abe Martin. Or maybe the other way around. I may be all mixed up, but look for the both of those.

Dick Cavett: Under one of those names we'll find him.

S. J. Perelman: Right.

Dick Cavett: Would you devise a "Must Read List" for a so-

called student of humor or do you have a series of books that you
find indispensable for the comic sensibility?

S. J. Perelman: Well, I think if anybody, Hubbard will probably
boil you down. Well, that is an invitation.

Dick Cavett: Take a chance.

S. J. Perelman: I think that anybody who wants to write owes it
to himself to read a marvelous book of Somerset Maugham's
called, *The Summing Up.* Do you know that book?

Dick Cavett: Yes, I do.

S. J. Perelman: I think if I were conceivably to teach rhetoric in
a school or university, I would insist that they read that book.

Dick Cavett: That was a partial biography written about thirty-
five years ago.

S. J. Perelman: That's right. And it contains some of the very
best advice ever given to would-be writers, but that's as a general-
ization.

Dick Cavett: For those who didn't catch the title, it's *The Summing Up.*

S. J. Perelman: Thank you.

Dick Cavett: I'm not implying that your diction needs improvement. It's just that people often say, "What was that book he said?"
and I just saved us a lot of letters. Well, this is almost an oneup-
manship thing to do, but I remember reading an interview you
gave and the writer was astonished that you spoke in sentences. It
seemed to have been written and polished and yet they were
definitely spontaneous. Is that an art that you can turn on and off
when you please?

S. J. Perelman: I usually speak a very rough mixture of New
Yorkese and with tags of Yiddish and other arcane languages.

Dick Cavett: Speaking of Yiddish, I must confess, being from
Nebraska, that I was about as what Mel Brooks called "spectacu-
larly gentile," but I was about a third of a way through a piece
where you were in Scotland before I realized that what appears
in print as a wonderful Scottish name, Gonich Konhilton is truly the
Yiddish phrase which one hears mispronounced occasionally.
Gonich Konhilton and so on and so on. And then all through the
piece you use those expressions. Now would you allow an anno-

tated Perelman for those who missed those things on first reading or do you figure they can fend for themselves?

S. J. Perelman: Well, I must say that was sort of industrial cavorting of some kind. I was in Scotland when it suddenly struck me that the name, MacManus, which is a common Scotch name is very much like the Yiddish word "Rachmanes," which means remorse. I lost my head and I started to translate every expression. For example, there is a remote village named Auchtatay in Scotland. Now, that's so much like "auchftenvey," which is kind of a breast beating expression that I seized on. And then, of course, with place names I'd easily follow the things like the star in "Chreckplatt" Pub, and all of that.

Dick Cavett: They worked beautifully.

S. J. Perelman: I'm afraid that I took unfair advantage of the reader. After all, he can get a Yiddish gloss anywhere in his neighborhood.

Dick Cavett: That's right. You have better things to do. Was it my misreading of it or did you find Tel Aviv a bit of a downer?

S. J. Perelman: Yes, I think that's one of the truly dreary places that I've ever been in. But in particular the hotel, which for the benefit of all is the Tel Aviv Hilton, and I say it loud and clear. That's the one that I worked out on, because I spent five wretched days there.

Dick Cavett: Is that the one you called the Xanadu?

S. J. Perelman: Yes, the Xanadu, yes. That really was about as rough an experience as I've ever had.

Dick Cavett: Was it everything from the concierge on up that bothered you?

S. J. Perelman: Well—

Dick Cavett: Do they have concierges there? They have them everywhere.

S. J. Perelman: I don't know.

Dick Cavett: That's French for janitor, isn't it?

S. J. Perelman: What you probably would call the concierge? I don't know what you would call them at the Tel Aviv Hilton.

Dick Cavett: I'm not sure.

S. J. Perelman: Something unprintable and inaudible, I would think.

Dick Cavett: I have a friend who's a kind of idiot savant on the subject of S. J. Perelman. He, for example, would say—how many instances can you think of where Perelman has wrought a variation on the phrase, "every prospect pleases an only man who's vial." I remember one at a dusty book store, Kahn's Bookstore, in which every prospect sneezes and only Kahn, the proprietor, only Mann, the proprietor—M-A-N-N.

S. J. Perelman: Mann, right.

Dick Cavett: Mann was vial. Yes, of course. I almost botched it for you. There are two or three that were discovered in the last couple books of yours I've read. At last count, how many times had you rendered that phrase?

S. J. Perelman: I don't know.

Dick Cavett: Are you aware of those things?

S. J. Perelman: Oh, I'm quite aware of it and I live and hope that I can torture a phrase once more. I see, by the way in this morning's *New York Times* that Russell Baker is fooling with a phrase that I use. I did a piece for the *New Yorker* recently about—about E.M. Forster's pants.

Dick Cavett: Being too short?

S. J. Perelman: That's right. What did I call the thing—a scram.

Dick Cavett: A scram, you made the pants too short.

S. J. Perelman: You made my pants too short. Well, Baker has got a variation of that. You've made the pains too short in this morning's *Times*. So, maybe we're in a kind of a lube contest with some kind.

Dick Cavett: You would think there would be enough phrases and clichés to go around. You were quoted somewhere recently as saying that the comic form is dying. Where do you see it surviving?

S. J. Perelman: Well, I have to say notably in someone you know very well and that's Woody Allen. I have high hopes that he, single-handed, may carry it on. Do you mean comic prose or . . .

Dick Cavett: I guess I mean comedy, in general. Would you value comic prose over, say, a movie like *Annie Hall*? If you were to tell Woody how to best spend his time, would you ask him to write more or make more films?

S. J. Perelman: Well, it would be a very hard choice, because I so enjoyed *Annie Hall*. I think I saw it three times. I think he's

done some astonishing things in that film. The business of having
Marshall McCluhan step out from behind the thing in the lobby—

Dick Cavett: And correct the bore—

S. J. Perelman: Yes, that's a real advance and in fact, the entire
scene, the conversation with the nudnick, and Woody's and Diane
Keaton's attempts to go on talking and fighting.

Dick Cavett: You sympathized with that, did you?

S. J. Perelman: And then I have to tell you that, although she
already had a very large place in my heart, Diane Keaton now is
a real threat to my sanity because that scene in which her girlish
glee in the scene with the lobsters . . . do you remember that?

Dick Cavett: Yes.

S. J. Perelman: Her enjoyment of his fright is absolutely masterly
or maybe mysteriously. I don't know.

Dick Cavett: It depends. Have you been to Hollywood yourself
lately? I know you once referred to the studio heads as men who had
four heads by electrolysis. Have you gone back?

S. J. Perelman: Only occasionally. The last chapter in this book
is when I completed my round.

Dick Cavett: That's the last time.

S. J. Perelman: That was the last time, yes.

Dick Cavett: In both senses of the phrase, the last time?

S. J. Perelman: No, no, no. I'm impelled every so often to go
back, out of real masochism, to torture one's self out there. I
find, by the way—have you ever tested this theory—that it's on the
twelfth day that you really go insane out there? I find that for
eleven days I would behave normally. I enjoyed the sunlight and the
people and all that, but I wake up on the morning of the twelfth
day with the secure knowledge that if I don't get out that day
something terrible may happen to me.

Dick Cavett: I wonder what it is about twelve days. Is it biblical?
Is it—it rings a bell somehow on the twelfth day. The twelfth day.

S. J. Perelman: That's right, it does. What would it be? Let's
leave it open and we'll think of it later.

Dick Cavett: Let's think about that, yes. But you've never felt
yourself succumbing to live there the way some people . . .

S. J. Perelman: No, I can't imagine any eventuality that however
dreadful would ever compel me to remain in that place.

Dick Cavett: I mean, what is there to occupy a Spanish house on the San Andreas Fault, for example, just for the sense of living on the edge and brink of calamity that seems to exhilarate so many people.

S. J. Perelman: No, I don't think that anything could possibly tempt me, though the place is full of friends of mine and very nice people. I just sit back East and brood about how they're managing. I suppose they are. They've reached the level of incomprehension or fright that allows them to just quietly go on living there.

Dick Cavett: Whatever it is, it worked. Is it any matter of our concern when we read you to know whether, for example in your book, the incident of the aphrodisiac that was sold to you as you were leaving—was it somewhere in Turkey or . . .

S. J. Perelman: I think it was Iran.

Dick Cavett: Whether that actually happened or not, is that any of the reader's business?

S. J. Perelman: You mean my statement to the effect that when a friend and I fettered to a rooster and job and the file exploded?

Dick Cavett: Yes, the ludicrous creature exploded in mid-air before our eyes.

S. J. Perelman: Yes. Well, I would hate to have to get up on the witness stand and placing one hand on the Bible swear that that actually happened.

Dick Cavett: Swear that you actually saw an exploding fowl.

S. J. Perelman: But the particular creep who presented me with this fetish, saying that this was the world's most powerful aphrodisiac, and I didn't have a chance to really test it.

Dick Cavett: That's what I was really after, the grain of truth in this that inspired the comic mind was that someone did present you with an aphrodisiac.

S. J. Perelman: Yes. This strange guy that I had met in Istahan, I think it was. But then I was one to test the aphrodisiac. For example, years ago, when I was in East Africa, I was given a slice of rhinoceros horn, which as you know, is greatly valued by the Chinese as an official aphrodisiac, but I never had the opportunity to put this to the test and I never could find any lady who would eat it, so there you are.

Dick Cavett: So, it remains untested in your mind.

S. J. Perelman: In my mind.

Dick Cavett: Well, I know it's decimated the rhinoceros population and apparently is of absolutely no value. So, don't rush out and get one.

S. J. Perelman: That's right, yes.

Dick Cavett: Yes. Are you still amused by your own work? I remember a wonderful line. You said as a young man you used to roll over and over marveling at the idiosyncrasies of the mind that had brought such gems. I hope that's an accurate quote.

S. J. Perelman: Yes. I think that every young writer values himself enormously in the absence of people valuing it for him.

Dick Cavett: I'm sorry to have to say that we're out of time. We never named the indispensable list of books. If you would send it to us, we'll publish it somehow to let the viewers know. Certainly, you should be on that list. And I can only say, goodbye to you now and see you again, I hope, another time.

S. J. Perelman: Thank you very much.

Dick Cavett: Thank you.

Perelman

Sukey Pett / 1978

From the Associated Press, 19 March 1978. By permission.

NEW YORK AP—Even for S. J. Perelman, who has traveled through Mau Mau country with an all-female safari and dotes on difficulties, the scene in Australia was a little trying.

Picture Perelman, one of the country's foremost comic writers, in an Australian airliner about to be hijacked. The stewardess announced: "If there are any people aboard who are subject to cardiac arrest, they'll be permitted to leave the aircraft."

Twenty-seven of the 35 passengers arose, including Perelman, but Perelman had a special dilemma. He had nine Ming plates, 15 inches in diameter, that he bought in Indonesia. How to get these valuable objects out of the plane when the passengers had to clamber out without benefit of ramp steps?

Perelman namely clambered out, with crockery intact. "I never wrote about it," he says, "because except for that one remark by the stewardess, it wasn't really funny. The hijacker was killed by the police, but not before he wounded a detective."

The humorously adventurous has seasoned Perelman's repertory for 40 years, through 21 books and innumerable articles in *The New Yorker*. His latest book, *Eastward Ha!* is a carousel about the rigorous eight months he spent traveling in Russia, Turkey, Greece, Scotland—and Hollywood.

"The point is," says Perelman, looking dashing, "that the commic writer is constantly searching for difficulties. One subjects himself to stress and difficulty that one can make copy out of. If your obligation is to amuse your readers, then you try to get into dilemmas that are grievous to yourself but not necessarily wounding or completely shattering."

Perelman's strenuous method has left him clearly unshattered. At 74, sitting in his apartment overlooking Gramercy Park, he is a picture of understated elegance: Average height, with graying hair and an immaculate dove-colored moustache. Those oval, steel-rimmed glasses he wears he brought back from Paris in 1927.

He was somewhat wounded, though, in the aftermath of the Australian hijack attempt a few years ago. The Ming plates he'd fretted over proved less precious than he had thought: When he sold them at Parke Bernet in New York, he lost $4 on the whole transaction.

Perelman speaks softly, slowly and precisely, reminiscing freely about Mau Mau country, Indonesia, and hijackings, but the interview starts in an unorthodox way.

"You've come to ask me questions," says Perelman, "so I have taken the liberty of preparing a few questions for you.

"1. If it's true, as his publishers contend, that Sidney Sheldon is the most gifted novelist since Victor Hugo, what is it about his work that rings your bell?

"2. If you had your druthers, which of the following would you prefer to be married to: George Brent; Max Schmeling; Evelyn Waugh; Donatello's statue of David?

"3. Hanes panty hose get loads of publicity because they are said to flatter a woman's legs. Why is it that I, who have flattered women's legs for years, get so little, publicity that is?"

Answer: How did you get into writing?

Unintentionally, it seems. Sidney Joseph Perelman, born in Brooklyn, "transported forcibly" to Providence, R.I., where he grew up, always wanted to be cartoonist. He drew for the humor magazine at Brown University and in his senior year was invited by *The Judge,* a well-known humor magazine, to drop in after graduation.

"I became very excited and saw visions of myself in a big studio surrounded by naked models and wearing a beret and Windsor tie," Perelman recalls, but when he went to New York the magazine didn't talk about a contract.

"I had a pretty thin time for a year and a half until I managed to start selling my work. About a year and a half later I began writing, which is a pretty natural transition for a comic artist."

A writer he remained, and among other things, he wrote numerous movie scripts, including the two Marx Brothers classics, *Horse Feathers* and *Monkey Business.* A typical Perelman line

forever identified with Groucho: Informed by his secretary that
"Jennings is waxing wroth outside," Groucho replies, "Well, tell
Roth to wax Jennings for a while."

One of Perelman's earlier literary creations, early '40s vintage,
was a private eye named Ian Turner. Dashiell Hammett around
that time wrote his first detective story, which gave it respectability,
but Perelman's great influence in those days was the pulp magazines,
"Spicy Detective" in particular.

"It was marvelous language," he recalls nostalgically, "because
everything counted . . . A roscoe pistol would bark or sneeze or
katchow. And there was the beginning of sex in those stories. The
man who wrote the Ian Turner stories juxtaposed the steely automatic
with the frilly panty and found that it paid off."

Sex is treated much more explicitly in print and in the movies
these days, and it prompts Perelman to summon up the wan ghost
of the Hayes office, at one time the guardian of taste and morals for
the film industry.

Completed scripts, he recalls, were sent to the Hayes office
before any footage was shot, and there was an imposing list of
taboos. You couldn't say, for example, "as poor as a church
mouse" because the office considered it a negative reflection
on religion.

"I was working on a script for Paramount. The hero and heroine
were riding horseback through Central Park. I wrote the scene
from the point of view of two Italian laborers who were discussing
the physical charms of the heroine. The scene was cut right out."

While Perelman wasn't fond of the Hayes office, he doesn't see
today's screen candor as an unmitigated blessing.

"The whole idea of full frontal nudity they've gotten to is the
absolute opposite of sex," he says. "The mystery is so much a
part of the process. It has been said, often by myself, that the flash
of garters in the Can-Can is far more exciting than frontal nudity
because it's the reserve that tickles."

And he muses about actresses.

"I think of Carole Lombard and Kay Kendall, two beautiful
women who—like Diane Keaton today—chose not to lean on their
beauty but to become comediennes, marvelous ones. There are all
these girls like Farrah Fawcett-Majors who, if they had the sense to

perceive it, would learn about comedy. Then they'd have a double punch. Most beauties forget that it takes talent and intelligence as well, which has to be supplemented by a lot of very hard work.''

New trends in writing. Perelman reflects a moment.

"Certainly the feminist novel is quite new. The language in those is pretty unbridled and the ladies all seem intent on trying to outdo Fanny Hill.

"I've read Erica Jong's *Fear of Flying* and *How to Save Your Own Life*. I think Erica Jong has shot her bolt, so to speak. We've retraced her career with her up to the present. I don't see how she can trade on this much longer. She regards herself as a very important personality. I caught a glimpse of her on the TV screen once and it struck me that she romanticizes her own beauty, to put it mildly.''

And what about the prolific Perelman's own output. It keeps happily growing, ''but I regret to say that I don't write every day anymore. I let myself drift through too much of the day for too many days.'' Perelman seems a little wistful and distant here.

"There's a question of momentum. If you let it die, it's much more of an effort to overcome the resistance. It's very arduous and painful and it should be a lesson to every writer, myself foremost, to keep on writing every day, otherwise you get terribly rusty.''

If there's rust in Perelman's polished prose, his many partisans would agree, it's not discernible to the naked eye.

From Paris to Peking with Perelman

Mary Blume / 1978

From The International Herald Tribune, 8 July 1978. Reprinted
by permission of Mary Blume.

London—In a few months if all goes well—and a lot of us are
cravenly hoping it won't go at all—the peasants of China will look
up from their rice paddies in astonishment at the sight of a jaunty
1949 MG YY Tourer (black, with red leather upholstery and Pennsylvania license plates) driven by a dapper gent in pebble glasses and
headed toward Peking.

The driver will be S. J. Perelman who, in the most flagrant
example of writer's masochism since Carlyle employed the wrong
maid, has decided to drive from Paris to Peking in the English
sports car he bought nearly 30 years ago in Bangkok at an
extremely favorable exchange rate. He intends to leave Sept. 1 and
live to write the tale for *London's Sunday Times,* providing what will
undoubtedly be the most significant commentary on the mysterious
East since "Chu Chin Chow."

Mr. Perelman oddly believes that the Chinese will be glad to fork
over the necessary visas and permits since he is perfectly willing
to carry two of them in the back seat of his roadster, where they
can watch him mesh gears to their hearts' content. Mr. Perelman
refuses to discuss his, it is said, utterly deniable skill at the wheel.
"Ask not what I can do for the MG but what the MG can do for
me," he replies with dignity.

He plans to follow what he describes as the southern route: Italy,
Yugoslavia, Bulgaria, Turkey, Iran, India, Burma, a boat to Hong
Kong and then Canton and Peking. He will be on the road three to
four months and is taking 30 boxes of Lomotil and 100,000
Bandaids. His trip has a historical precedent: In 1907, Prince
Borghese drove from Peking to Paris, a thoroughly harrowing
journey. "They did it the hard way. If there is a hard way," Mr.
Perelman says.

Mr. Perelman's first long trip was as a tot from his native
Providence, R.I. all the way to New York. "I think I took jelly
sandwiches in waxed paper that my mother had prepared and I
imagine as we passed Fall River my eyes sparkled because the Lizzie
Borden legend was still alive." Mr. Perelman still has a sneaking
fondness for that youthful ax killer. "Aug. 4, 1982. The hottest
day of the year. Aug. 4 is always the hottest day of the year. And
they sat down to a breakfast of warmed-over mutton soup, cold
mutton and fried bananas. No wonder."

Since that early trip. Mr. Perelman has suffered from what he
calls travel sickness. "Loathesome as travel is," he says. "I've
become hooked on it." He has been around the world in all
conceivable directions and had come to London to abet the
publication of his latest book. *Eastward Ha!* (an earlier trip in which
he circumscribed the globe the other way was called *Westward
Ha!*). In London he moved out of his usual haunt, which he refers
to as Brown's Hotel for Distressed Gentlewomen, to teeming South
Kensington in preparation for the trip. Here he can be found at the
formica-topped tables on what he describes as bizarre nookleter-
ias: "I've been doing a little training here in the Arab restaurants
chewing through the kebabs," he says.

Mr. Perelman's female friends not only worry for his safety on
the spin to Peking; they are also jealous. He used to travel with a
hairy cartoonist named Al Hirschfeld, who limned the master in
poses that may have been fetching but were unsatisfying clothes-
wise. "For some reason Mr. Hirschfeld always represents me as
looking like a pool hustler," Perelman complains.

Mr. Hirschfeld did not accompany Mr. Perelman when the latter
decided, unaccountably, a few years ago to go around the world
in 80 days, his place being taken by a vapid brunette whom Mr.
Perelman jettisoned in Hong Kong (she later resurfaced to work
for Dinah Shore). On the China trek he will be accompanied by a
dimpled blonde amazon recommended by a lady who has written
biographies of Jayne Mansfield and Louisa May Alcott.

"The blonde amazon's name is Delta Willis. She's roughly 6-
foot-2 and she's from Pine Bluff, Arkansas." Mr. Perelman says.
Miss Willis has been working as vice president of a company called
Survival Anglia, Ltd., and she wants really to go to Kenya. Mr.

Perelman claims he has told her it is not on the route. Her job will be to change tires, clean sparkplugs, mother the motor and ride shotgun. Mr. Perelman, gripping the wheel, says he will stop for nothing.

"In case I am pursued by brigands," he gallantly says, "I intend to throw portions of this lady to impede them as I hurtle on."

Perelman in Cloudsville

Mel Calman / 1978

From *Sight & Sound* vol. 47, 4 August 1978:248–9. Reprinted by permission.

Perelman: I first went out to Hollywood in December 1930, as I recall, soon after Groucho had hired Will Johnstone and me to work on *Monkey Business*. It began when I went to a performance of *Animal Crackers* on Broadway, and I was so entranced that I went to see them after the show. Groucho explained to me that the group was interested in doing some radio. The odd thing is that Johnstone was then a working newspaper cartoonist. I myself had worked for five years, both drawing and writing for *Judge* and the old *Life* magazine. We were both essentially comic artists.

Johnstone had worked for the Marx Brothers before, on a vaudeville sketch. Johnstone and I got into a huddle in a room for three days and the only idea we came up with was the notion of the four Marxists as stowaways on a transatlantic liner—each one in his own barrel. Having thought of this, our inspiration completely gave out. On the third day the Marx Brothers rang up and asked us to lunch. We put forward this idea and to our complete stupefaction Groucho turned to Chico and said, 'This isn't a radio sketch, boys—this is our next picture.' And before we had recovered our breath they took us by the hand and led us to the Paramount Building and introduced us to Jesse Lasky. We were both signed to six week contracts at 500 dollars a week. For us this was big money.

The Marx Brothers departed to Europe to appear at the London Palladium and we started work on the screenplay. Our supervisor was a man called Herman Mankiewicz (author with Welles of the screenplay of *Citizen Kane*). He was a Teutonic, overbearing broth of a man who was famous for his cutting wit. An interesting thing about the word 'supervisor'. The men who dominated movies had all been either pack peddlers or junk dealers. Sam Goldwyn had been a glove-maker. Mayer was a junk dealer. And the term 'supervisor' was a factory term.

Johnstone and I sat down and wrote what we thought was a screenplay. Neither one of us was experienced in this form; but we had picked up a lot of very professional terms—dollies, iris out and so forth—and we thought it necessary to cram all this nonsense into the script. There was a thing known as the Vorkapich shot. This was invented by a man named Vorkapich, who was a special effects man at Paramount. It was a fast close-up (like a zoom) to the face. Well, we Vorkapiched all over the place. We thought in our innocence that all these instructions would act as a guide to the director. We wrote about 125 pages in this fashion.

> (The Marx Brothers had a disastrous season in London and returned to Hollywood. They summoned Perelman and Johnstone to read the script to them.)

There were the three married Marxes and their wives. They had also picked up some dogs—huge creatures. And their father . . . and their dentist, their lawyers, and their accountants. And Herman Mankiewicz and his wife, and his brother. There were 29 people and three dogs in that room. I began to read the script and I read all the instructions as well as the dialogue. When I got through there was a considerable silence. Chico turned to Groucho and said, 'Well, what do you think?' Groucho said audibly. 'Stinks'. Everybody rose and slowly left the room.

We went home and told our wives to start packing. The next morning the phone rang and Groucho said, 'Come over and let's get to work.' It took us about six months to write a new script and that became *Monkey Business*.

Did they add suggestions while you were writing it?

Largely speaking, Harpo and Chico were only interested in their specialties. Groucho was concerned in the whole picture . . . He considered me to be too literary. He often hurled this charge at me. For instance—in that picture Groucho and Thelma Todd were making love and I had written the scene so that suddenly Groucho was to jump up and say, 'Come Kapellmeister, let the violas throb, my regiment leaves at dawn.' And then he was to go into a

parody of the famous scene from *The Merry Widow*. Groucho
read this scene and said, 'The trouble is that the barber in Peru
won't get it.' He meant Peru, Indiana. I disagreed violently with
him, because I think that Groucho was a master of parody. What
eventually happened was that this whole scene was cut out. But
that one line is still in the picture. It always gives me a thrill to hear
that line.

Didn't you work on another Marx Brothers film?

Yes. Eighteen months later they hired me to work on *Horse
Feathers* in collaboration with Kalmar and Ruby. But the Marxes
were boorish, they were ungrateful. It was a very uneasy combination. Harpo was the nicest brother.

In 1934 my wife (who was Nathanael West's sister) and I had
written our first play, which was made into a picture. I went back
to Hollywood whenever we were broke. Hollywood could absorb
writers. There were five big studios. The studios owned the
cinemas and the bill was changed twice a week, so that an enormous
amount of product was needed. There were at one time 104
writers on the lot at Metro. All of us were on an assembly line,
rewriting each other's pictures. After the first novelty, working
there quickly became very boring. I began to see that it was a
technique, that anyone of reasonable intelligence could pick up.
What films were about then—and what, I think, films are still
about—was the unexpected. Those people prospered who had a quick
mind and the ability to arrange shallow, trivial situations that were
unexpected. It is a medium in which a lot of shallow people became
successful.

What did you think of Irving Thalberg? Was he impressive?

My wife and I worked on one picture for Thalberg and I never
saw any sign of this greatness. He was able to buy talent. I can
remember when eight of the most famous playwrights in America
were in his anteroom, waiting to see him. It was my first intimation of
what power means. In my mind, power is the ability to purchase
people and make them wait for you.

Didn't you work on Sweethearts? *That seems a rather unlikely
film for you to have been involved in.*

We were hired by Thalberg to work on this wretched thing called *Greenwich Village,* which was an almost indescribable pot-pourri of nonsense. Later on we were hired by Hunt Stromberg to work on *Sweethearts* . . . There is always a courtship period between a producer and a writer, in which the producer asks the writer what he wants to work on. This is as formalised a ritual as a bullfight. If the writer is naive at all (and he usually is), he comes up with a suggestion. We suggested a play and related the plot to Stromberg. Stromberg countered by asking if we had heard of *Arms and the Man.* He wanted to combine *Arms and the Man* with *The Chocolate Soldier.*

By the way, he said—speaking of Victor Herbert, have you heard of *Sweethearts?* At this our eyes capsized in our heads because some of the sickliest music that has ever been written is that stuff. He then got hold of a record player and played some of this dreadful hogwash. That's what we're going to make, as though the idea had just appeared, like a Mazda bulb over his head. Well, we needed the work. We needed the money. So we numbly acceded. We figured we could dress it up. You always think . . . well . . . things are bad . . . but you have to eat. We stuffed a psychiatrist into it . . . all kinds of things. My wife was then heavily pregnant with our first child and she had begun to show, so we finally told Stromberg that she couldn't continue working on the picture. She retired from the scene and he hired Dorothy Parker and her husband, Alan Campbell.

Stromberg became intensely creative. He used to walk up and down, dictating voluminous notes about the characters. Dorothy Parker sat, knitting a long shapeless garment that eventually became about 14 feet long and two feet wide. It looked like a carpet for a staircase. She had those Winston Churchill glasses perched on the end of her nose and a look of . . . she was way off in some other country. Her husband was a beautiful looking man—a great conference man, always popping ideas. Every so often Stromberg would stop and say, 'Dorothy, what do you think of it so far?' And she'd look up over the top of her glasses and say, 'Oh, I do think it's marvellous, don't you?' Later on, they wrote *A Star is Born*—the one with Fredric March.

What was the average salary in Hollywood then?

The Screenwriters Guild made a study in 1935 and found that the average salary was 30 dollars a week. Because some writers were working for nothing—right up to Ben Hecht who was getting 5,000 dollars a week. But the average was probably somewhere between 500 and 1,750 dollars a week. Successful writers like the Hacketts (who wrote *The Thin Man* movie) were making around $5,000 a week. All our salaries, by the way, were common gossip. It was that kind of society. The social life consisted of interminable dinner parties where nothing was talked about but film. Grosses, performances. It was like an industrial town where shoes are made . . . and where nothing but shoes is talked about.

Dorothy Parker referred to it as fairy money, which disappeared before you ever left the town. And it did—in a strange way. Those of us who came from the East went out there in a buccaneering spirit. We didn't care to live in those palaces . . . we just wanted to earn a quick dollar in order to get on with our own work.

Interview with S. J. Perelman
Dick Cavett / 1978

From *The Dick Cavett Show*, 12 May 1978. Guest: S. J. Perelman. Published by permission of Daphne Productions.

Dick Cavett: Good evening. When they gave out the National Book Awards recently here in New York, they added, for the first time, a special achievement medal, honoring an excellent and sustained contribution to world literature.

Well, the deserving recipient was my guest tonight, Mr. S. J. Perelman and I don't know what the citation said, but it was probably a lot more solemn and a lot less funny than a note about the author that appeared in one of Mr. Perelman's books about twenty years ago.

Let me read it to you. It said, this is on the dust jacket, "S. J. Perelman is S. J. Perelman, which is an extravagant compliment in itself. In the words of one who knew him well or as well as he wanted to know him, just before they made S. J. Perelman, they broke the mold." I've been very fond of that. Is it fair or square to ask you who actually authored those words about you?

S. J. Perelman: I don't really remember. I think it could have been Groucho Marx or it may have been George Kaufman.

Dick Cavett: Could it even have been yourself?

S. J. Perelman: That's a strong possibility. I've been known to make up my own blurbs, yes.

Dick Cavett: Speaking of Kaufman, one of my favorite blurbs that he wrote for you is the obligatory appreciation. I think I mentioned this the last time you were here. It says, "In appreciation of S. J. Perelman, by George S. Kaufman" and the eye drops down to a single line of type which is "I appreciate S. J. Perelman."

S. J. Perelman: Yes.

Dick Cavett: I guess that put appreciations where they belong for all time.

S. J. Perelman: I think so, yes.

Dick Cavett: Mr. Perelman, I don't know if you'll accept this primness, but it seems to me that your working principal, and you stated this, is to put yourself in an anguishing situation. We've read pieces that you've written in climates hot and scalding, in miserable hotels and awful parts of the world and your idea seems to be that this produces art for you, sometimes. I think you said there's a residue that can be turned into comic fiber.

S. J. Perelman: Well, it's all based on the principle of *Schadenfreude,* you know. Joy in someone else's suffering. I think we all relish discomfort on the part of even our best friends, and I think that the reader gets a proper satisfaction and a rather warm glow out of a spectacle of someone caught in an intangible situation.

Dick Cavett: I wonder if you going on television the same way, is that something you put yourself through or can you actually enjoy it?

S. J. Perelman: Well, don't you know, the whole business of writers on television was all started by a man, who we both knew, whose name has just . . .

Dick Cavett: Alexander King.

S. J. Perelman: That's right. And as you recall, searching around for a quick guest, Jack Parr latched onto Alex King, whose book had appeared months before and had just dropped dead. There was never any review because it came out during a strike and all that sort of thing. And of course, Alex got on this thing and figuring that his book had no chance whatever he attacked the Catholic Church with great virulence completely stumping Jack Parr and the audience. They turned to stone and Alex finished off. And finally, Parr held up the book and said, ''I don't really know who this man is but I think he's written a very, very funny book.'' And within about three or four weeks, the book took off and just began selling like crazy.

Dick Cavett: Yes, that started a lot of things. That was the first they realized that the power of TV would sell a book, apparently.

S. J. Perelman: Right.

Dick Cavett: And also it began publishers urging their authors to cultivate television personalities.

S. J. Perelman: And from then on, you know, it's been impossible to get as much as an ad of that size out of publishers. They say, ''Well, if you want exploitation, you've just got to go on the road.''

And people like Jackie Suzanne, just crisscross the United States, in fact, this hemisphere and the other one.

Dick Cavett: Yes, she practically sold her book door-to-door. It was admirable, heroic in a way. She went from town to town. She wouldn't apparently turn away any literary teas, any autograph parties; any place they would have her and some places where she wasn't even expected, I think, she showed up.

S. J. Perelman: That's right.

Dick Cavett: Well do you do that? Do you do that?

S. J. Perelman: No. I've been persuaded at the point of a dagger to go to Boston and Washington and so forth, but I don't really relish it and it just seems to me that the work involved in writing, in the first place, should at least be a release from that kind of thing. But I know that a great many writers do enjoy it.

Dick Cavett: Like to hit the road and become, in a way, performers. They get to crave the audience.

S. J. Perelman: They do.

Dick Cavett: You wrote once, somewhere, that writers often don't have the performing ability. People expect them to, expect them to run around the stage like a Marx brother, I think you said. But it isn't necessarily the same gift, by any means.

S. J. Perelman: No, not at all. There's a complete division between the comic writer and the performer, and I think that it's a great mistake to expect more of the writer than he can give.

Dick Cavett: Have you had that experience with meeting your heroes in the writing field and had that feeling of it's not possible that this drab personality I'm meeting could possibly have written that sparkling prose.

S. J. Perelman: That's right. It has happened to me and I'm sure that it constantly happens.

Dick Cavett: I don't know what you can do about it, but there is a tremendous pressure on writers to go on television and some of them have better personalities on television than they do in the ring. It can work the other way around, too.

S. J. Perelman: Yes. Mostly the whole cult of personality was founded by people like Leonard Lyons, Walter Winchell and the columnists. It's much more pronounced in this country than it is in Europe, for example.

Dick Cavett: Whom do we have to thank for that, besides those columnists? Is it some national appetite for just celebrity for its own sake, no matter . . .

S. J. Perelman: Yes. The hoards of autograph seekers, that's characteristic. Just like the people lounging around outside Sardi's in the evening, just hoping and scanning every face for some clue to . . . it's celebrity.

Dick Cavett: Have you ever been asked if you were anybody? In so many words, "Are you anybody?"

S. J. Perelman: No, but I'm sure that you're constantly subjected to this, aren't you?

Dick Cavett: Yes. Well, usually, they get my name. Sometimes they'll say Dick Clark when they're being overcome with emotion in saying it.

S. J. Perelman: Or Dick Cabbage.

Dick Cavett: But are you anybody? I have heard people ask, which is a little insulting because you suddenly check to see if you cast a shadow when they say, "Are you anybody?"

S. J. Perelman: Yes, I was once riding in a large vehicle to attend an opening night at the Egyptian Theatre on Hollywood Boulevard with some quite noted actress and faces suddenly began peering into the window asking whether we were anybody. But fortunately, she was an actress of the silent screen somewhat older than myself, so that nobody remembered either her or myself.

Dick Cavett: It's terrible to be asked that. It's like saying, "Do you exist?"

S. J. Perelman: That's right.

Dick Cavett: Your brother-in-law was Nathanael West, author of *Miss Lonelyhearts* and *Day of the Locust,* two novels that have had a kind of cult following over the years, but though most people are probably familiar with the movie of *Day of the Locust.* And in that final scene where there's the fire and the mob and outside Grauman's Chinese, I realize that there's a moment in your writing, at some point, where you said, "I was watching"—where it says in effect: "I was watching the dignitaries of Hollywood drive up in limousines and so on and I fully expected God and his raft to obliterate the whole shah-bang," almost as if you foresaw this. Well, I don't know which came first, as a matter of fact.

S. J. Perelman: Well, of course, out of our close friendship, going all the way back to the time when we both attended Brown University, West and I were concerned with matters like that and more so in Hollywood when we were both there together, but I think that final scene that you speak of came out very badly on television. I thought that the picture itself illustrated the usefulness of trying to convert an interesting book into a film, which was demonstrated again by that lack of success with Gatsby. They tried Gatsby—I won't say innumerable times, but several times—and it's never worked.

Dick Cavett: Can you say why it is?

S. J. Perelman: Yes, because I think that there are imponderables in a novel that can't be translated. They approached this particular novel, *The Day of the Locust* with great reverence. [John] Schle-singer told me years before that he was crazy about the book and they got a first-rate screen writer, Waldo Salt, to work on it and they spent a great deal of money on it, but it just didn't work anymore than the last *Great Gatsby* did.

Dick Cavett: There's something mysterious about the art of the novel, apparently. You think what you're getting is visual, but it's probably more than visual. It's something else.

S. J. Perelman: Yes, and I think almost the very best films have come from something that was written for the medium.

Dick Cavett: Although maybe *Gone with the Wind* was better than the book. Who knows?

S. J. Perelman: Well, that's true, but something like *Double Indemnity* for instance,—well, that was originally written by Jim Cain as a novel, wasn't it or as a story?

Dick Cavett: I'm not sure. I thought it was an original screenplay, but I don't know why I thought that. I think you're right.

S. J. Perelman: Yes, and then Raymond Chandler worked on the screenplay at least and Billy Wilder and Charlie Brackett pro-duced it, but it was entirely the work of people who were working in Hollywood.

Dick Cavett: Did you know Chandler?

S. J. Perelman: Yes, I did. I got to know him towards the end of his life.

Dick Cavett: He's a strange man. I've only recently begun to read his books, *Lady in the Lake* and some of those things, and they're way beyond what you just think of as detective stories.

S. J. Perelman: Oh, they are, yes, they're a product of intense work, you know. The seeming effortlessness that you get is completely wrong because he wrote version after version.

Dick Cavett: Did he?

S. J. Perelman: And he told me once that—I think, we had been sufficiently involved with a certain gin drink so that we were exchanging this sort of information—he said that the thing he detested and was most frightened of was the blank sheet of paper. That he used to lure himself in a room with a tape recorder and talk endless nonsense into it just trying to get some sort of idea and he would have these things typed up. He would do this three or four times and finally take the product to his typewriter and write his first rather painful version of the book and this went on. He would do about six or seven versions of that.

Dick Cavett: I find that astonishing, because for one to be able to talk into a tape recorder uninhibitedly would be one thing, but knowing somebody's going to see it and type it up for you, would take a lot of courage.

S. J. Perelman: Yes, but it took that kind of courage and work to produce expressions like, "as dapper as a French Count in a college play." I mean he describes how Marlow shuts the screen door. He says, "Shut the door as carefully as though it were made of short pie crust."

Dick Cavett: Short pie crust.

S. J. Perelman: Yes.

Dick Cavett: Well, there are wonderful lines in it. You think they ought to be in Bartlett's quotations, practically, they're so good. And Chandler, I think he's probably underestimated—and it does read effortlessly, almost as in a sort of throw away that Bogart played Marlow on the screen. You can almost hear Bogart's line.

S. J. Perelman: That's right.

Dick Cavett: He seems to be a very strange man. He liked cats and he married a much older woman, apparently, a much older woman.

S. J. Perelman: That's right, and it was her death that really unhinged him. It was after her death that he began drinking to excess and he attempted suicide, which was not successful, but the whole product of his self-destruction finally became clear and he died, I think, a matter of two years after she.

Dick Cavett: He wrote *The Blue Dahlia,* I believe. Did he? The screenplay for that movie?

S. J. Perelman: Yes.

Dick Cavett: And some other screenplays.

S. J. Perelman: He detested Hollywood, actually. He was very unhappy there. He was a strange man.

Dick Cavett: I wonder if you were at the writer's table that he refers to when—I think there's a book called, *Raymond Chandler Speaking*—in which he talks about his experiences in Hollywood, and he said the wit at the writer's table was wonderful. They were discussing a well-known movie actress, whose name I won't mention, and a younger man said: "The way you're talking about her, would you be willing to say she's a nymphomaniac?" And the other writer said, "Well, I suppose she would be if you could calm her down a little." Were you present when that was said?

S. J. Perelman: No, I wasn't, but it sounds very much like Harry Kurnitz, whom you may have known.

Dick Cavett: Kurnitz, yes. By the way, you realize that you're revered, don't you and that there are people who . . .

S. J. Perelman: By whom?

Dick Cavett: Well . . .

S. J. Perelman: Someone hiding in the shadows here?

Dick Cavett: When I've had you on in the past, I've gotten the most grateful mail from people saying, thank you for bringing us S. J. Perelman. Almost as if I had performed some miracle. But one of the things that I think no one could know is how good you are at writing. Is it called the dedication? You know, when you sign a book to somebody and they say, write something in the front, is there a word for that? The sentiment, perhaps.

S. J. Perelman: Yes.

Dick Cavett: Well, I picked up a book once. I don't think you know what I'm going to say, belonging to Patricia Neal. You had given it to her. And at the point where people usually write, most authors came up with something like, good luck or something, you had, "To Pat . . ." I don't want to get it wrong. "To Pat: This extravagant gala entry conceived in anguish, executed in want and remaindered in toto,'' which to me is a tiny masterpiece. Do you have those ready?

S. J. Perelman: Well, I don't but since you've mentioned her name, a friend of mine always contended that every man is in love with two women. His wife and Patricia Neal.

Dick Cavett: And you can verify that?

S. J. Perelman: Yes, I can.

Dick Cavett: Okay. Are you obsessed with dry cleaners or is it just my imagination? Ever since I began reading Perelman, going back through no starch in the dhoti and what's the one that contains the line, ''Rose—Rose''—what is it? ''Rose Finkel, Rose Finkel, why don't you marry this woman if you love her so much?''

S. J. Perelman: That's called Eine Kleine MothMusik.

Dick Cavett: Eine Kleine MothMusik, yes.

S. J. Perelman: Yes. I am, but I think that most are obsessed with dry cleaners or laundrymen because just think of the inter-relation of the dry cleaner with yourself. I mean, he, after all, is the man who crushes your buttons beyond repair or presses them into the fabric so, there's a white spot on the lapel, you know. And he's the man, who with infinite ingenuity causes those little saw teeth in your collar and shrinks your clothes so you can't get them on. I mean, I think the laundrymen and the dry cleaner are very, very close to you. Maybe much closer than a psychiatrist.

Dick Cavett: To our true being?

S. J. Perelman: Right.

Dick Cavett: We all know they're humorless people and they're people who don't laugh. I think it's a rare, odd thought. Are there humorless countries, as well, in your experience? You are one of the most well-traveled men in the world.

S. J. Perelman: Yes, I think that there are principally two, Germany and France.

Dick Cavett: Really?

S. J. Perelman: Yes, I think that both of those countries are very deficient in this respect because I think that the English and ourselves—we like humor and we practice it because a great part of it consists in self-deprecation and the Germans never deprecate themselves.

Dick Cavett: They find nothing to laugh about in the subject of themselves?

S. J. Perelman: No, and the French are essentially pompous. The thing that we value in English humor and in our own is the spectacle of ourselves caught in impossible circumstances involved with machines that don't function, with people, with home—to homes we can't relate. I mean, that kind of inefficacy is very important in humor.

Dick Cavett: So, have France and Germany produced any humorous writers of great note in recent years? I mean, were there great wits of the French in the past with respect to—

S. J. Perelman: The French, of course, have produced great wits and great epic masters, but the Germans have produced no considerable body of humor.

Dick Cavett: It occurred to me the other day that no one anywhere, in anything I have ever read about Hitler has ever intimated that he had anything resembling a sense of humor. There's nothing even purporting to be a humorous remark by him. Perhaps this is not surprising. But you would think that somewhere, somebody would have said that he made at least what he thought was a joke, which was such and such.

S. J. Perelman: Yes, and most German laughter is evoked by the spectacle of people rather cruelly involved, that is to say, slipping on the banana peel kind of thing. That gets an awful lot of buffs in the father land.

Dick Cavett: Buffs by the rhyme. Except for a piece you wrote, I think called, "Meanness Rising in the Suds" about soap operas recently in the *New Yorker,* I think that's about the the first time I've seen you make much use of television. Although you do draw on what you call the crafts and vulgar occasionally for your inspiration, but do you own a television? Do you sit in front of the box in horror?

S. J. Perelman: Always.

Dick Cavett: Is it meat for your—I was going to say meat for your mill, grist for your grinder to remix the metaphor.

S. J. Perelman: Well, I, I watch annually; I bathe in the delights of the Academy Awards. I really think that $400 or whatever a television set costs is a small price to pay for the delights of that one evening.

Dick Cavett: What amuses you? What do you enjoy so about it?

S. J. Perelman: Well, the gratitude that people display to their family, their bookmaker, heaven knows what for the success that they—I also love to watch them plunging towards the rostrum, you know, with the chest foremost and that glitter in the eye. And then, of course, the oscillation—the kissing that goes on among the bestowers and the receivers and what not.

Dick Cavett: Do you think that's where Oscar comes from? Oscillation? But somehow I doubt it; I don't think so.

S. J. Perelman: Should we have a moment of silence, Dick?

Dick Cavett: I'm terribly sorry. Yes.

S. J. Perelman: To mark the death of that one.

Dick Cavett: We have one, whether we want to or not. You see, I think it's always a good idea to add that there's no audience here, in case people think we're playing for laughs and bombing.

S. J. Perelman: Yes, that's true.

Dick Cavett: It's always good to say that. I picture you working over your material several times. You said that West did that or Chandler. And somewhere I ran across this, I would love to know where this comes from. Do you know where Mark Twain says, "The difference between the right word and the almost right word is the difference between the lightning bug and the lightning?"

S. J. Perelman: No, I've heard that once before.

Dick Cavett: Would it be embarrassing to ask you how many typed pages you turn out a day of your so-carefully perfected work?

S. J. Perelman: Well, it's embarrassing, but I'll twist my own wrist and tell you that it's a big day when I can get a page out. I mean, it—but then you know there are different methods of writing among comic writers. Thurber, for example, used to write very swiftly a complete version of whatever he wrote. He would probably do ten or twelve of those, but there are others, drudges like myself, who pause over the sentence and try to get all the words right before going onto the next one.

Dick Cavett: The first time you go from word to word, practically.

S. J. Perelman: That's right, yes. The trouble with that form of writing is that you lose track of what's coming up in the future, and also you can be diverted from the central track very easily so you go off on angles. But then that's useful for me, too, because on the principle that one words reminds me of another, I may get somewhere. But it's a great deal like wading through a swamp without high rubber boots.

Dick Cavett: Are people still saying, did you get started on that novel? I know you've said in the past you're content to stitch at your embroidery hoop, and you reject the idea that bigger is better and that Thomas Wolfe should be considered better than Robert Benchley, but aren't you tempted to try to add to that very small list you have made of comic novels that are truly comic novels in the world?

S. J. Perelman: Well, my second book, years and years ago was a collaboration with Quentin Reynolds, the famous reporter and we wrote a prohibition novel back in the early '30s, which was called *Parlor, Bedlam and Bath*. This was based upon a famous play many years before called *Parlor, Bedroom and Bath*. And we wrote this together and it perished like a dog. That cured me of any ambitions to write a novel. However, I am often reminded that I ought to be getting along with an autobiography. I don't know. There's a compulsion on the part of people to have you write an autobiography when you get older, and I have tapped away at it and I think that I'm on page 35 now, but I've been on page 35 for quite a few years.

Dick Cavett: There are plenty of us who would be grateful for even 34 pages. I do hope you'll continue to page 36, at least, before you throw the whole thing away. There's so many more things I still want to talk to you about, but unfortunately, time has done it's dirty work to us. So, it's been a pleasure and an honor as always and may the sadistic dry cleaner not get his clutches on you.

S. J. Perelman: Thank you. It's always great fun for me.

One Kaddish, Sunny Side Up, and Hold the Lachrymae

Alan Coren / 1979

From *Punch*, 24 October 1979. Reprinted by permission.

It's taken me ten months to work up a decent rage about the absence of *The Times,* and it cost the death of a short exophthalmic genius three thousand miles away to do it.

Yesterday, even as the serried illiterates sat facing one another across the No Man's Land of the Gray's Inn Road negotiating table, sullenly snarling the clichés of industrial jargon which were putting the final twist of the garotte around the Thunderer's debilitated glottis, Sidney Joseph Perelman was himself quietly slipping away in an upstairs room of the Gramercy Park Hotel, New York. And what fills me with fury this morning is that, due to the ongoing confrontational deadlock situation, the Great Master of the English Word has no *Times* for his obituary.

There is nowhere that Sid would have rather had his leavetaking appear. In that bizarre romantic anglophilia of his, he would have relished the idea of antique retainers ironing the paper in their butler's pantries before hobbling up the Grinling Gibbons staircases to lay it beside the master's kedgeree; or the thought of crumpled copies lying around the Athenaeum and the Reform, on cracked leather arms and Regency side-tables, one or two, perhaps, covering the faces of wizened bishops with curious names; or the vision of this sheet or that blowing down Burlington Arcade and fetching up against the premises of a swordstick factor, a cobbler of rustic brogues, and importer of hand-rolled Burmese stogies.

We used to meet for tea, Sid and I, at Brown's Hotel, during his years of exile in a London that never came up to his impossible Edwardian expectations, and eat cucumber sandwiches the size of Cape triangulars. I don't think either of us liked them much, but ritual has nothing to do with personal fancies, or communion wafers would come with raisins in. Sid liked to sit in a hermetically enclosed

pocket of Old Mayfair, watching frail dowagers from the shires mur-
muring to and fro. That he could watch the toing and the froing at the
same time, at least apparently, had much to do with the fact that his
eyes pointed different ways, one could never be quite certain just
how much of his attention one was commanding. He thought about
them a lot, his eyes; indeed, about his appearance generally, and
was much given to describing it: "a balding, presbyopic individual
with a ragged handlebar moustache and a complexion the colour of
beetroot." He hated the way he looked; he once murmured to me
(everything was murmured; I used to walk beside him with a
permanent list towards the moving mouth beneath) in Sulka's, whither
we had repaired (his words) to buy six pairs of dress socks: "I never
get over the shock of being Rex Harrison inside and then catching
sight of myself in one of these damn mirrors."
    We looked at him, then, in the glass, and I had the impression of a
small military man, the martinet-in-chief of some courageous, smart,
yet very short regiment. He had clipped his moustache, and it turned
up slightly at the ends; he wore thornproof tweeds and a checked
shirt and a striped quasi-collegiate tie. A foot taller, and he could have
been a retired Grenadier colonel; perhaps even an Uhlan—those fine
mad words of his floated into my head, from one of his *Cloudland
Revisited* extravaganzas in which he confessed that, for some time
after seeing Erich von Stroheim in *Foolish Wives,* "I exhibited a
maddening tendency to click my heels and murmur *Bitte?* along
with a twitch as though a monocle were screwed into my eye. The
mannerisms finally abated, but not until the Dean of Brown University had taken me aside and confided that if I wanted to transfer to
Heidelberg, the faculty would not stand in my way."

    That wild incongruity between the ego-ideal of the English coun-
try gentleman and the reality of the Brooklyn-born son of pogrom-
fleeing immigrants was, of course, something of which Sid was
constantly aware, and constantly on the *qui vive* to ridicule. We were
once strolling down Constitution Hill together, on an especially
English spring morning, engaged in a slightly precious discussion
anent, as I dimly remember, some claret that he intended buying
for no better reason than the pleasure he took in visiting St. James's
wine-merchants, when, from the direction of Buckingham Palace

came the clatter of the Household Cavalry in the process of changing themselves. Whereupon Sid suddenly clutched my arm, and, in a rare shout, cried: "Cossacks! Run for your life!"

And again, a couple of weeks later, he turned up for a Wednesday lunch here at *Punch,* full of quiet glee, and carrying a curious walking-cane which he informed was a Penang lawyer, an item once used by British planters to settle industrial disputes. He had bought it an hour or so before at John Smith, the Holborn stick-maker, and, having paid for it, had given it an imperial swish and said to the assistant: "Not much call for these today, eh, my boy?" To which, and to Sid's delight, the man had replied: "On the contrary, sir, you're the thirteenth American this morning."

It informed his miraculous prose, all this. Critics prepared to take the crazy risk of analyzing humour have, from time to time, rattled on about S. J. Perelman's acid wit, his immaculate ear, his bottomless vocabulary, his visionary extravagance, and so forth, and true enough it all is; but for me, what sets him apart from the other comic masters (and mistress) of the *New Yorker's* lost heyday is the extraordinary deft elegance of his line and rhythm, those fine periods that bear you along until the shock of a lunatic quirk, when Henry James collides with Groucho Marx, when the dandy with the Penang lawyer looks in the mirror and sees, aghast, the kid from Washington Heights.

I can actually remember not only discovering Perelman, but also the first paragraph of his I ever read; and also what it did to me. The reminiscences of better hacks than I tend to teem with momentous pubescent confrontations, when, in those formative years prior to the setting of ambition's jelly, they suddenly fall upon *The Waste Land or Emma or Nostrome* and thereafter spend the next few weeks mooning about in literary shock, determined upon a career behind the quill, as novelist, poet, playwright, or whatever. I read a lot of smart stuff in my teens, but it never happened to me, although I desperately wanted it to; I had, that is, immortal longings in me I wished to satisfy in words, but never found a form to charge me. I did not close *The Prelude* or *Vanity Fair* and burn to go and do likewise. Until—I was fourteen—a *New Yorker* found its unlikely way into our house, God knows how, and I read: "I guess I'm not an old mad scientist at bottom. Give me an under-

ground laboratory, half a dozen atom smashers, and a beautiful
girl in a diaphanous veil waiting to be turned into a chimpanzee, and
I care not who writes the nation's laws.''

And that was more or less that. For several months following, I
not only read all the Perelman I could lay my hands on, I also
wrote enough of it to fill a medium-sized incinerator. He was not an
easy man to find: suburban libraries had not heard of him,
bookshops sent me curtly away to look up the name again and come
back when I had it right, and newsagents carried only spasmodic
issues of *The New Yorker,* many of which I forked out good dinner-
money for, only to find that they contained no Perelman whatever and
were instead lined from wall to wall with numbingly dull stories
about growing up in either Maine or North Carolina. And then
Crazy Like A Fox came out, in Penguin. I have it before me as I
write: it cost something called 2/6, and I have to open it with care,
because it's been opened a thousand times before, and the yellowed
pages drop, now, from the gumless spine, and form new conjunc-
tions on the floor, which is fine for the worthless junk of William
Burroughs but no fate for the impeccable precision of Sid.

It took me long years to control the writing hold he had over me,
and I wasn't alone, God knows, in that; there's a lot of Perelman
in a lot of humorists, how could there not be, but after a while, if
you're lucky, the influence diffuses through your stuff, flavours
it, and you stop writing second division Perelman; you find, if you
can, your own voice and accept with pleasure those slight inflec-
tions in it whose provenance is unmistakable. A couple of years
ago—I tell this bit with awkwardness and considerable embarrass-
ment, but I want to tell it for a number of reasons, and there's only
one way of getting into it—the *New York Times* wrote a flattering
review of a book of mine which contained the unnerving phrase,
''he is the natural heir to Perelman.''

Hardly were the copies cold before I received a cable from Sid: I
SEE SOME CAD HAS LET SLIP YOUR MOTHERS DARK
SECRET STOP DON'T THINK THIS ENTITLES YOU TO A
LIEN ON MY ESTATE STOP MY LAWYERS ARE IN THE
MAIL.

It was too late. I already had the inheritance. I hope I don't
squander it, but even if I do, it won't matter too much. The
original gold is still there, in a dozen books, and it will not tarnish.

Index